# A CRITIQUE
# OF
# INTERVENTIONISM

# A CRITIQUE OF INTERVENTIONISM

## LUDWIG von MISES

RLINGTON HOUSE·PUBLISHERS
NEW ROCHELLE, NEW YORK 10801

Originally published in 1929 as *Kritik des Interventionismus* and republished in 1976 under the same title and incorporating the essay "Nationalization of Credit?" Copyright © 1929 and 1976 by Gustav Fischer Verlag. "Nationalization of Credit?" first appeared in the *Journal of National Economics*, vol. I, 1930 (copyright Springer-Verlag, Wien).

Translation copyright © 1977 by Margit von Mises

Manufactured in the United States of America


**Library of Congress Cataloging in Publication Data**

Von Mises, Ludwig, 1881-1973.
  A critique of interventionism.

  Translation of Kritik des Interventionismus.
  1.  Austrian school of economics.  2.  Economics.
I.  Title.
HB98.V6313   1977       330.15'7      77-24186
ISBN 0-87000-382-8

# CONTENTS

# FOREWORD

My husband wrote the essays in this book in the early 1920s, more than fifty years ago. They were collected and published as an anthology in 1929 by Gustav Fischer, formerly in Jena, now in Stuttgart, under the title *Kritik des Interventionismus*. Although these articles deal with the economic problems of that day, the same problems are still with us, perhaps in an even more serious and menacing way than ever.

The book has recently been republished in Germany by the Wissenschaftliche Buchgesellschaft in Darmstadt, with a preface by my husband's friend and former student, the illustrious Professor F. A. von Hayek, 1974 Nobel laureate in economics. The new German edition includes the essay "The Nationalization of Credit?" which also appears in this translation.

I am very happy that this book is now being made available in English. I am no economist, but I have gone over the German and English texts of these essays, and I congratulate Professor Hans F. Sennholz, whom I asked to do the translation, for his brilliant work. He has done a remarkable job of transposing the lengthy, complicated sentences—so typical of the German language of the 1920s—into fluent and elegant English. I am proud to see my husband's work presented in this form to a new audience, and I hope it will be read widely.

MARGIT VON MISES

7

# INTRODUCTION

We may grow in knowledge of truth, but its great principles are forever the same. The economic principles that Ludwig von Mises expounded in these six essays during the 1920s have endured the test of time, being as valid today as they were in the past. Surely, the names and places have changed, but the inescapable interdependence of market phenomena is the same today, during the 1970s, as it was during the 1920s, and as valid for present-day Americans as it was for the Germans of the Weimar Republic.

And yet, most social scientists today are as ignorant of this interdependence of economic phenomena as they were during the 1920s. They are statists, or as Professor Mises preferred to call them, "etatists," who are calling upon government to assume ever more responsibilities for the economic well-being of its citizens. No matter what modern economists have written about the general validity of economic laws, the statists prefer their ethical judgments over economic principles, and political power over voluntary cooperation. Without government control and regulation, central planning and authority, they are convinced, economic life would be brutal and chaotic.

In this collection of essays Ludwig von Mises emphasizes again and again that society must choose between two systems of social organization: either it can create a social order that is built on private property in the means of production, or it can establish a command system in which government owns or manages all production and distribution. There is no logical third system of a private property order subject to government regulation. The "middle of the road" leads to socialism because government intervention is not only superfluous and useless, but also harmful. It is superfluous be-

9

cause the interdependence of market phenomena narrowly circumscribes individual action and economic relations. It is useless because government regulation cannot achieve the objectives it is supposed to achieve. And it is harmful because it hampers man's productive efforts where, from the consumers' viewpoint, they are most useful and valuable. It lowers labor productivity and redirects production along lines of political command, rather than consumer satisfaction.

And yet, most American economists tenaciously cling to their faith in the middle of the road with all its government regulations and controls. Like the German "Socialists of the Chair," whose doctrines face Professor von Mises' incisive critique in these pages, American "mainstream" economists are seeking the safety of an impartial middle position between classical liberalism and communism. But while they may feel safe on the middle of the road, hopefully equally distant from the competing systems, they are actually paving the way for socialism.

Paul A. Samuelson, the "mainstream economist" par excellence, devotes his *Economics* (New York: McGraw-Hill Book Co., 1976), the textbook for millions of students, to modern post-Keynesian political economy, whose fruits, according to the author, are "the better working of the mixed economy" (p. 845). Like the Socialists of the Chair long before him, he simply ignores "conservative counterattacks against mainstream economics." He neither defines nor describes these attacks, which he repels with a four-line gesture of disgust after he announces them in a boldface title. With selfishness, ignornace, and malice "there is not much intellectual arguing that can be done" (p. 847).

He devotes half a page to the "Chicago School Libertarianism" of men like Frank Knight, Henry C. Simons, Friedrich Hayek, and Milton Friedman. And like the Socialists of the Chair, he merely labels pleas for individual freedom and the private property order as "provocative negations." His favorite target, Milton Friedman, is dispatched with an ugly joke: "If Milton Friedman had never existed, it would have been necessary to invent him" (p. 848).

10

But the champions of all-round government ownership or control in the means of production are treated with utmost courtesy and respect. He devotes eight pages of text supplemented by eight pages of appendix to "eminent," "competent," and "eloquent" advocates of radical economics from Karl Marx to John G. Gurley. He quotes extensively from their writings without refuting any of their arguments. To Samuelson, as to the Socialists of the Chair, Karl Marx "was as much a philosopher, historian, sociologist, and revolutionist. And make no mistake. He was a learned man" (p. 855). In fact, Samuelson echoes Engels: "Marx was a genius . . . the rest of us were talented at best" (p. 853).

If this is the middle of the road, or "mainstream economics," the future of the American private property system is overshadowed by the dark clouds of Marxian doctrine and policy. This is why Ludwig von Mises' *Critique of Interventionism* is as pertinent and timely today as it was half a century ago.

HANS F. SENNHOLZ

11

# PREFACE

The fighting between nations and states, and domestically between political parties, pressure groups, and cliques, so greatly occupies our attention that we tend to overlook the fact that all the fighting parties, in spite of their furious battling, pursue identical economic objectives. We must include here even the advocates of a socialization of the means of production who, as partisans of the Second International and then the Third International with its approval of the New Economic Policy (NEP), at least for the present and near future renounced the realization of their program. Nearly all writers on economic policy and nearly all statesmen and party leaders are seeking an ideal system which, in their belief, is neither capitalistic nor socialistic, is based neither on private property in the means of production nor on public property. They are searching for a system of private property that is hampered, regulated, and directed through government intervention and other social forces, such as labor unions. We call such an economic policy *interventionism*, the system itself the *hampered market order*.

Communism and fascism are in agreement on this program. The Christian churches and various sects concur with the Moslems of the Middle East and India, the Hindus, Buddhists, and the followers of other Asiatic cultures. And anyone reflecting upon the programs and actions of the political parties of Germany, Great Britain, and the United States must conclude that differences exist only in the methods of interventionism, not in its rationale.

In their entirety the following five essays and articles constitute a critique of interventionist policies and their under-

13

lying ideologies. Four of them have been published in recent years—three in journals and one in the *Handbook of Social Sciences*. The second essay deals with Professor Schmalenbach's recent theories, among other things, and is published here for the first time.

Ludwig von Mises

*Vienna*
*June 1929*

# INTERVENTIONISM[1]

## 1.
## Interventionism as an Economic System

Ever since the Bolshevists abandoned their attempt to realize the socialist ideal of a social order all at once in Russia and, instead, adopted the New Economic Policy, or NEP, the whole world has had only one real system of economic policy: interventionism. Some of its followers and advocates are thinking of it as a temporary system that is to be replaced sooner or later with another order of the socialist variety. All Marxian socialists, including the Bolshevists, together with the democratic socialists of various persuasions, belong to this group. Others are holding to the belief that we are dealing with interventionism as a permanent economic order. But at the present this difference in opinion on the duration of interventionist policy has only academic significance. All its followers and advocates fully agree that it is the correct policy for the coming decades, yea, even the coming generations. And all agree that interventionism constitutes an economic policy that will prevail in the forseeable future.

Interventionism seeks to retain private property in the means of production, but authoritative commands, espe-

1. *Archiv für Sozialwissenschaft und Sozialpolitik* [Archives for social science and social policy], vol. 36, 1926.

cially prohibitions, are to restrict the actions of private owners. If this restriction reaches the point that all important decisions are made along lines of authoritative command, if it
is no longer the profit motive of landowners, capitalists, and
entrepreneurs, but reasons of state, that decide what is to be
produced and how it is produced, then we have socialism
even if we retain the private property label. Othmar Spann
is completely correct when he calls such a system "a private
property order in a formal sense, but socialism in substance."[2] Public ownership in the means of production is
nothing but socialism or communism.

However, interventionism does not want to go that far. It
does not seek to abolish private property in production; it
merely wants to limit it. On the one hand, it considers un-
limited private property harmful to society, and on the other
hand, it deems the public property order unrealizable completely, at least for the present. Therefore, it seeks to create
a third order: a social system that occupies the center between the private property order and the public property
order. Thus, it seeks to avoid the "excesses" and evils of
capitalism, but to retain the advantages of individual initiative and industry which socialism cannot bring forth.

The champions of this private property order, which is
guided, regulated, and controlled by the state and other social organizations, are making demands that have always
been made by political leaders and masses of people. When
economics was yet unknown, and man was unaware that
goods prices cannot be "set" arbitrarily but are narrowly determined by the market situation, government commands
sought to regulate economic life. Only classical economics
revealed that all such interventions in the functioning of the
market can never achieve the objectives which the authorities aim to achieve. The old liberalism which built its economic policies on the teachings of classical economics therefore categorically rejected all such interventions. *Laissez faire
et laissez passer!* Even Marxian socialists have not judged interventionism any differently from the classical liberals.

---

2. Othmar Spann, *Der wahre Staat* [The true state], Leipzig, 1921, p. 249.

They sought to demonstrate the absurdity of all interventionist proposals and labeled them contemptuously as "bourgeois." The ideology that is swaying the world today is recommending the very system of economic policy that is rejected equally by classical liberalism and older Marxism.

# 2.
# The Nature of Intervention

The problem of interventionism must not be confused with that of socialism. We are not dealing here with the question of whether or not socialism in any form is conceivable or realizable. We are not here seeking an answer to the question of whether human society can be built on public property in the means of production. The problem at hand is, What are the consequences of government and other interventions in the private property order? Can they achieve the result they are supposed to achieve?

A precise definition of the concept "intervention" is now in order.

1. Measures that are taken for the purpose of preserving and securing the private property order are not interventions in this sense. This is so self-evident that it should need no special emphasis. And yet it is not completely redundant, as our problem is often confused with the problem of anarchism. It is argued that if the state must protect the private property order, it follows that further government interventions should also be permissible. The anarchist who rejects any kind of state activity is said to be consistent. But he who correctly perceives the impracticability of anarchism

and seeks a state organization with its apparatus of coercion in order to secure social cooperation is said to be inconsistent when he limits government to a narrow function.

Obviously, this reasoning completely misses the point. We are not here discussing the question of whether or not social cooperation can do without the organization of coercion, which is the state, or government. The sole point under discussion is whether there are only two conceivable possibilities of social organization with division of labor, that is, the public property order and the private property order—disregarding syndicalism—or whether there is yet a third system as assumed by interventionists, namely, a private property order that is regulated through government intervention. Incidentally, we must carefully distinguish between the question of whether or not government is necessary and the question of where and how government authority is in order. The fact that social life cannot do without the government apparatus of coercion cannot be used to conclude also that restraint of conscience, book censorship, and similar measures are desirable, or that certain economic measures are necessary, useful, or merely feasible.

Regulations for the preservation of competition do not at all belong to those measures preserving the private property order. It is a popular mistake to view competition between several producers of the same product as the substance of the ideal liberal economic order. In reality, the central notion of classical liberalism is private property, and not a certain misunderstood concept of free competition. It does not matter that there are many recording studios, but it does matter that the means of record production are owned privately rather than by government. This misunderstanding, together with an interpretation of freedom that is influenced by the natural rights philosophy, has led to attempts at preventing the development of large enterprises through laws against cartels and trusts. We need not here discuss the desirability of such a policy. But we should observe that nothing is less important for an understanding of the economic effects of a certain measure than its justification or rejection by some juristic theory.

Jurisprudence, political science, and the scientific branch of politics cannot offer any information that could be used for a decision on the pros and cons of a certain policy. It is rather unimportant that this pro or that con corresponds to some law or constitutional document, even if it should be as venerable and famous as the Constitution of the United States of America. If human legislation proves to be ill-suited to the end in view, it must be changed. A discussion of the suitability of policy can never accept the argument that it runs counter to statute, law, or constitution. This is so obvious that it would need no mention were it not for the fact that it is forgotten time and again. German writers sought to deduce social policy from the character of the Prussian state and "social royalty." In the United States, economic discussion now uses arguments that are derived from the Constitution or an interpretation of the concepts of freedom and democracy. A noteworthy theory of interventionism set forth by Professor J. R. Commons is largely built on this rationale and has great practical significance because it represents the philosophy of the La Follette party and the policy of the state of Wisconsin. The authority of the American Constitution is limited to the Union. But locally the ideals of democracy, liberty, and equality reign supreme and give rise, as we can observe everywhere, to the demand for abolition of private property or its "limitation." All this is insignificant for our discussion and, therefore, does not concern us here.

2. Partial socialization of the means of production is no intervention in our sense. The concept of intervention assumes that private property is not abolished, but that it still exists in substance rather than merely in name. Nationalization of a railroad constitutes no intervention; but a decree that orders an enterprise to charge lower freight rates than it otherwise would is intervention.

3. Government measures that use market means, that is, seek to influence demand and supply through changes of

market factors, are not included in this concept of intervention. If government buys milk in the market in order to sell it inexpensively to destitute mothers or even to distribute it without charge, or if government subsidizes educational institutions, there is no intervention. (We shall return to the question of whether the method by which government acquires the means for such actions constitutes "intervention.") However, the imposition of price ceilings for milk signifies intervention.

*Intervention is a limited order by a social authority forcing the owners of the means of production and entrepreneurs to employ their means in a different manner than they otherwise would.* A "limited order" is an order that is no part of a socialist scheme of orders, i.e., a scheme of orders regulating all of production and distribution, thus replacing private property in the means of production with public property. Particular orders may be quite numerous, but as long as they do not aim at directing the whole economy and replacing the profit motive of individuals with obedience as the driving force of human action they must be regarded as limited orders. By "means of production" we mean all goods of higher order, including the merchants' inventories of ready goods which have not yet reached the consumers.

We must distinguish between two groups of such orders. One group directly reduces or impedes economic production (in the broadest sense of the word including the location of economic goods). The other group seeks to fix prices that differ from those of the market. The former may be called "restrictions of production"; the latter, generally known as price controls, we are calling "interference with the structure of prices."[3]

---

3. There may be some doubt about the suitability of a third group: interference by taxation which consists of expropriation of some wealth or income. We did not allow for such a group because the effects of such intervention may in part be identical with those of production restrictions, and in part consist of influencing the distribution of production income without redirecting production itself.

# 3.
# Restrictions of Production

Economics need not say much about the immediate effect of production restrictions. Government or any organization of coercion can at first achieve what it sets out to achieve through intervention. But whether it can achieve the remoter objectives sought indirectly by the intervention is a different question. And it must further be determined whether the result is worth the cost, that is, whether the intervening authority would embark upon the intervention if it were fully aware of the costs. An import duty, for instance, is surely practical, and its immediate effect may correspond to the government's objective. But it does not follow at all that the import duty can realize the government's ultimate objective. At this point the economist's work commences. The purpose of the theorists of free trade was not to demonstrate that tariffs are impractical or harmful, but that they have unforeseen consequences and do not, nor can they, achieve what their advocates expect of them. What is even more significant, as they observed, protective tariffs as well as all other production restrictions reduce the productivity of human labor. The result is always the same: a given expenditure of capital and labor yields less with the restriction than without it, or from the beginning less capital and labor is invested in production. This is true with protective tariffs that cause grain to be grown in less fertile soil while more fertile land is lying fallow, with class restrictions of trade and occupation (such as the certificates of qualification for certain occupations in Austria, or the favored tax treatment of small enterprises) which promote less productive businesses at the expense of more productive ac-

21

tivity, and, finally, with the limitation of labor time and of the employment of certain labor (women and children), which diminishes the quantity of available labor.

It may very well be that government would have intervened even with full knowledge of the consequences. It may intervene in the belief that it will achieve other, not purely economic, objectives, which are thought to be more important than the expected reduction in output. But we doubt very much that this would ever be the case. The fact is that all production restrictions are supported wholly or partially by arguments that are to prove that they raise productivity, not lower it. Even the legislation that reduces the labor of women and children was enacted because it was believed that only entrepreneurs and capitalists would be handicapped while the protected labor groups would have to work less.

The writings of the "Socialists of the Chair" have been rightly criticized in that, in the final analysis, there can be no objective concept of productivity and that all judgments on economic goals are subjective. But when we assert that production restrictions reduce labor productivity, we do not yet enter the field where differences in subjective judgments prohibit observations on the goals and means of action. When the formation of nearly autarkic economic blocs hampers the international division of labor, preventing the advantages of specialized large-scale production and the employment of labor at the most advantageous locations, we face undesirable consequences on which the opinions of most inhabitants of the earth should not differ. To be sure, some may believe that the advantages of autarky outweigh its disadvantages. In the discussion of the pros and cons its advocates brazenly assert that autarky does not diminish the quantity and quality of economic goods, or else they do not speak about it openly and clearly. Obviously, they are fully aware that their propaganda would be less effective if they were to admit the whole truth of the consequences.

All production restrictions directly hamper some production inasmuch as they prevent certain employment opportunities that are open to the goods of higher order (land, capital, labor). By its very nature, a government decree that "it be" cannot create anything that has not been created before. Only the naive inflationists could believe that government could enrich mankind through fiat money. Government cannot create anything; its orders cannot even evict anything from the world of reality, but they can evict from the world of the permissible. Government cannot make man richer, but it can make him poorer.

With most production restrictions this is so clear that their sponsors rarely dare openly claim credit for the restrictions. Many generations of writers, therefore, sought in vain to demonstrate that production restrictions do not reduce the quantity and quality of output. There is no need to deal again with the protective tariff arguments that are raised from a purely economic point of view. The only case that can be made on behalf of protective tariffs is this: the sacrifices they impose could be offset by other, noneconomic advantages—for instance, from a national and military point of view it could be desirable to more or less isolate a country from the world.[4]

Indeed, it is difficult to ignore the fact that production restrictions always reduce the productivity of human labor and thus the social dividend. Therefore, no one dares defend the restrictions as a separate system of economic policy. Their advocates—at least the majority of them—are now promoting them as mere supplements to government interference with the structure of prices. The emphasis of the system of interventionism is on price intervention.

---

4. For a critique of these notions see my *Nation, Staat und Wirtschaft* [Nation, state and economy], Vienna, 1919, p. 56 *et seq.*, especially with regard to German policies since the 1870s.

# 4.
# Interference with Prices

Price intervention aims at setting goods prices that differ from those the unhampered market would set.

When the unhampered market determines prices, or would determine prices if government had not interfered, the proceeds cover the cost of production. If government sets a lower price, proceeds fall below cost. Merchants and producers will now desist from selling—excepting perishable goods that quickly lose value—in order to save the goods for more favorable times when, hopefully, the control will be lifted. If government now endeavors to prevent a good's disappearance from the market, a consequence of its own intervention, it cannot limit itself to setting its price, but must simultaneously order that all available supplies be sold at the regulated price.

Even this is inadequate. At the ideal market price supply and demand would coincide. Since government has decreed a lower price the demand has risen while the supply has remained unchanged. The available supply now does not suffice to satisfy the demand at the fixed price. Part of the demand will remain unsatisfied. The market mechanism, which normally brings demand and supply together through changes in price, ceases to function. Customers who were willing to pay the official price turn away in disappointment because the early purchasers or those who personally knew the sellers had bought the whole supply. If government wishes to avoid the consequences of its own intervention, which after all are contrary to its own intention, it must resort to rationing as a supplement to price controls and selling orders. In this way government determines the quantity that may be sold to each buyer at the regulated price.

A much more difficult problem arises when the supplies

that were available at the moment of price intervention are used up. Since production is no longer profitable at the regulated price, it is curtailed or even halted. If government would like production to continue, it must force the producers to continue, and it must also control the prices of raw materials, semifinished products, and wages. But such controls must not be limited to a few industries which government meant to control because their products are believed to be especially important. The controls must encompass all branches of production, the prices of all goods and all wages, and the economic actions of all entrepreneurs, capitalists, landowners, and workers. If any industry should remain free, capital and labor will move to it and thus frustrate the purpose of government's earlier intervention. Surely, government would like an ample supply of those products it deemed so important and therefore sought to regulate. It never intended that they should now be neglected on account of the intervention.[5]

Our analysis thus reveals that in a private property order isolated intervention fails to achieve what its sponsors hoped to achieve. From their point of view, intervention is not only useless, but wholly unsuitable because it aggravates the "evil" it meant to alleviate. Before the price was regulated, the economic good was too expensive in the opinion of the authority; now it disappears from the market. But this was not the intention of the authority seeking to lower the price for consumers. On the contrary, from its own point of view, the scarcity and inability to find a supply must appear as the far greater evil. In this sense it may be said that limited intervention is illogical and unsuitable, that the economic system that works through such interventions is unworkable and unsuitable, and that it contradicts economic logic.

---

5. On the effectiveness of price controls versus monopolistic prices see my "Theorie der Preistaxen" [Theory of price controls] in *Handwörterbuch der Staatswissenschaften* [Handbook of social sciences], 4th ed., vol. VI, p. 1061 *et seq.* The essay appears below in this collection. To understand price controls as they are directed at monopolistic prices, we must not be influenced by popular terminology that detects "monopolies" everywhere, but work rather with the strictly economic concepts of monopoly.

If government is not inclined to alleviate the situation through removing its limited intervention and lifting its price control, its first step must be followed by others. Its decree that set price ceilings must be followed not only by decrees on the sale of all available supplies and the introduction of rationing, but also price controls on the goods of higher order and wage controls and, finally, mandatory labor for businessmen and workers. And such decrees must not be limited to a single or a few industries, but must cover all branches of production. There is no other choice: government either abstains from limited interference with the market forces, or it assumes total control over production and distribution. Either capitalism or socialism; there is no middle of the road.

Let us take yet another example: the minimum wage, wage control. It is unimportant whether government imposes the control directly, or labor unions through physical coercion or threats prevent employers from hiring workers who are willing to work for lower wages.[6] As wages rise, so must the costs of production and also prices. If the wage earners were the only consumers as buyers of the final products, an increase in real wages by this method would be inconceivable. The workers would lose as consumers what they gained as wage earners. But there are also consumers whose income is derived from property and entrepreneurial activity. The wage boost does not raise their incomes; they cannot pay the higher prices and, therefore, must curtail their consumption. The decline in demand leads to dismissal of workers. If the labor union coercion were ineffective, the unemployed would exert a labor market pressure that would reduce the artificially raised wages to the natural market rate. But this escape has been closed. Unemployment, a friction phenomenon that soon disappears in an

---

6. It should be noted that we are not dealing here with the question of whether or not wage rates can be raised permanently and universally through collective bargaining, but with the consequences of a general wage boost achieved artificially through physical coercion. To avoid a theoretical difficulty pertaining to money, namely that a general rise in prices is impossible without a change in the ratio between the quantity of money and its demand, we may assume that together with the boost in wages a corresponding reduction in the demand for money takes place through a reduction in cash holdings (e.g., as a result of additional paydays).

unhampered market order, becomes a permanent institution in interventionism.

As government did not mean to create such a condition, it must intervene again. It forces employers either to reinstate the unemployed workers and pay the fixed rate, or to pay taxes that compensate the unemployed. Such a burden consumes the owners' income, or at least reduces it greatly. It is even conceivable that the entrepreneurs' and owners' income no longer can carry this burden, but that it must be paid out of capital. But if nonlabor income is consumed by such burdens we realize that it must lead to capital consumption. Capitalists and entrepreneurs, too, want to consume and live even when they are earning no incomes. They will consume capital. Therefore, it is unsuitable and illogical to deprive entrepreneurs, capitalists, and land owners of their incomes and leave control over the means of production in their hands. Obviously, the consumption of capital in the end reduces wage rates. If the market wage structure is unacceptable the whole private property order must be abolished. Wage controls can raise rates only temporarily, and only at the price of future wage reductions.

The problem of wage controls is of such great importance today that we must analyze it in yet another way, taking into consideration the international exchange of goods. Let us suppose that economic goods are exchanged between two countries, Atlantis and Thule. Atlantis supplies industrial products, Thule agricultural products. Under the influence of Friedrich List,* Thule now deems it necessary to build its own industry by way of protective tariffs. The final outcome of Thule's industrialization program can be no other than that fewer industrial products are imported from Atlantis, and fewer agricultural products exported to Atlantis. Both countries now satisfy their wants to a greater degree from domestic production, which leaves the social product smaller than it used to be because production conditions are now less favorable.

This may be explained as follows: in reaction to the import duties in Thule the Atlantean industry lowers its

*Editor's note: A nineteenth century (1789–1846) German advocate of the use of protective tariffs to stimulate national industrial development.

27

wages. But it is impossible to offset the whole tariff burden through lower wages. When wages begin to fall it becomes profitable to expand the production of raw materials. On the other hand, the reduction in Thulean sales of agricultural products to Atlantis tends to lower wages in the Thulean raw material production, which will afford the Thulean industry the opportunity to compete with the Atlantean industry through lower labor costs. It is obvious that in addition to the declining capital return of industry in Atlantis, and the declining land rent in Thule, wage rates in both countries must fall. The decline in income corresponds to the declining social product.

But Atlantis is a "social" country. Labor unions prevent a reduction in wage rates. Production costs of Atlantean industry remain at the old pre-import-duty levels. As sales in Thule decline Atlantean industry must discharge some workers. Unemployment compensation prevents the flow of unemployed labor to agriculture. Unemployment thus becomes a permanent institution.[7]

The exportation of coal from Great Britain has declined. Inasmuch as the unneeded miners cannot emigrate—because other countries do not want them—they must move to those British industries that are expanding in order to compensate for the smaller imports that follow the decline in exports. A reduction in wage rates in coal mining may bring about this movement. But labor unions may hamper this unavoidable adjustment for years, albeit temporarily. In the end, the decline in the international division of labor must bring about a reduction in standards of living. And this reduction must be all the greater, the more capital has been consumed through "social" intervention.

Austrian industry suffers from the fact that other countries are raising their import duties continually on Austrian products and are imposing ever new import restrictions,

---

7. On the question of how collective bargaining can temporarily raise wage rates see my essay "Die allgemeine Teuerung im Lichte der theoretischen National-ökonomie" [The high costs of living in the light of economic theory] in vol. 37 of *Archiv*, p. 570 *et seq.* On the causes of unemployment see C. A. Verrijn Stuart, *Die heutige Arbeitslosigkeit im Lichte der Weltwirtschaftslage* [Contemporary unemployment in the light of the world economy], Jena, 1922, p. 1 *et seq;* L. Robbins, *Wages,* London, 1926, p. 58 *et seq.*

such as foreign exchange control. Its answer to higher duties, if its own tax burden is not reduced, can only be the reduction in wages. All other production factors are inflexible. Raw materials and semifinished products must be bought in the world market. Entrepreneurial profits and interest rates must correspond to world market conditions as more foreign capital is invested in Austria than Austrian capital is invested abroad. Only wage rates are determined nationally because emigration by Austrian workers is largely prevented by "social" policies abroad. Only wage rates can fall. Policies that support wages at artificially high rates and grant unemployment compensation only create unemployment.

It is absurd to demand that European wages must be raised because wages are higher in the U.S. than in Europe. If the immigration barriers to the U.S., Australia, et cetera, would be removed, European workers could emigrate, which would gradually lead to an international equalization of wage rates.

The permanent unemployment of hundreds of thousands and millions of people on the one hand, and the consumption of capital on the other hand, are each consequences of interventionism's artificial raising of wage rates by labor unions and unemployment compensation.

# 5.
# Destruction Resulting from Intervention

The history of the last decades can be understood only with a comprehension of the consequences of such intervention in the economic operations of the private property order. Since the demise of classical liberalism, interventionism has been the gist of politics in all countries in Europe and America.

The economic layman only observes that "interested parties" succeed again and again in escaping the strictures of law. The fact that the system functions poorly is blamed exclusively on the law that does not go far enough, and on corruption that prevents its application. The very failure of interventionism reinforces the layman's conviction that private property must be controlled severely. The corruption of the regulatory bodies does not shake his blind confidence in the infallibility and perfection of the state; it merely fills him with moral aversion to entrepreneurs and capitalists.

But the violation of law is not an evil that merely needs to be eradicated in order to create paradise on earth, an evil that flows from human weakness so difficult to uproot, as etatists so naively proclaim. If all interventionist laws were really to be observed they would soon lead to absurdity. All wheels would come to a halt because the strong arm of government comes too close.

Our contemporaries view the matter like this: farmers and milk dealers conspire to raise the price of milk. Then comes the state, the welfare state, to bring relief, pitting common interest against special interest, public economic view against private point of view. The state dissolves the "milk cartel," sets ceiling prices, and embarks upon criminal prosecution of the violators of its regulations. The fact that milk does not become as cheap as the consumers had wished is now blamed on the laws that are not strict enough, and on their enforcement that is not severe enough. It is not so easy to oppose the profit motive of pressure groups that are injurious to the public. The laws must therefore be strengthened and enforced without consideration or mercy.

In reality, the situation is quite different. If the price ceilings were really enforced, the delivery of milk and dairy products to the cities would soon come to a halt. Not more, but less milk, or none at all, would come to the market. The consumer still gets his milk only because the regulations are circumvented. If we accept the rather impermissible and fallacious etatist antithesis of public and private interests, we would have to draw this conclusion: the milk dealer who violates the law is serving the public interest; the government official who seeks to enforce the ceiling price is jeopardizing it.

Of course, the businessman who violates the laws and regulations in order to produce regardless of government obstacles is not guided by considerations of public interest, which the champions of the public interest belabor continually, but by the desire to earn a profit, or at least to avoid the loss which he would suffer complying with the regulation. Public opinion, which is indignant at the baseness of such motivation and the wickedness of such action, cannot comprehend that the impracticability of the decrees and prohibitions would soon lead to a catastrophe were it not for this systematic disregard of government orders and prohibitions. Public opinion expects salvation from strict compliance with government regulations passed "for the protection of the weak." It censures government only because it is not strong enough to pass all necessary regulations and does not entrust their enforcement to more capable and incorruptible individuals. The basic problems of interventionism are not discussed at all. He who timidly dares to doubt the justification of the restrictions on capitalists and entrepreneurs is scorned as a hireling of injurious special interests or, at best, is treated with silent contempt. Even in a discussion of the methods of interventionism, he who does not want to jeopardize his reputation and, above all, his career must be very careful. One can easily fall under the suspicion of serving "capital." Anyone using economic arguments cannot escape this suspicion.

To be sure, public opinion is not mistaken if it scents corruption everywhere in the interventionist state. The corruptibility of the politicians, representatives, and officials is the very foundation that carries the system. Without it the system would disintegrate or be replaced with socialism or capitalism. Classical liberalism regarded those laws best that afforded least discretionary power to executive authorities, thus avoiding arbitrariness and abuse. The modern state seeks to expand its discretionary power—everything is to be left to the discretion of officials.

We cannot here set forth the impact of corruption on public morals. Naturally, neither the bribers nor the bribed realize that their behavior tends to preserve the system which public opinion and they themselves believe to be the right one. In violating the law they are conscious of impairing the public weal. But by constantly violating criminal laws and moral decrees they finally lose the ability to distinguish between right and wrong, good and bad. If finally few economic goods can be produced or sold without violating some regulation, it becomes an unfortunate accompaniment of "life" to sin against law and morality. And those individuals who wish it were different are derided as "theorists." The merchant who began by violating foreign exchange controls, import and export restrictions, price ceilings, et cetera, easily proceeds to defraud his partner. The decay of business morals, which is called "inflation effect," is the inevitable concomitant of the regulations that were imposed on trade and production during the inflation.

It may be said that the system of interventionism has become bearable through the laxity of enforcement. Even the interferences with prices are said to lose their disruptive power if the entrepreneurs can "correct" the situation with money and persuasion. Surely, it cannot be denied that it would be better without the intervention. But, after all, public opinion must be accommodated. Interventionism is seen as a tribute that must be paid to democracy in order to preserve the capitalistic system.

This line of reasoning can be understood from the viewpoint of entrepreneurs and capitalists who have adopted Marxian-socialistic or state-socialistic thought. To them, private property in the means of production is an institution that favors the interests of landowners, capitalists, and entrepreneurs at the expense of the public. Its preservation solely serves the interests of the propertied classes. So, if by making a few painless concessions these classes can salvage the institution that is so beneficial to them, and yet so harmful to all other classes, why jeopardize its preservation by adamantly refusing the concessions?

Of course, those who do not share this view regarding "bourgeois" interests cannot accept this line of thought. We do not see why the productivity of economic labor should be reduced through erroneous measures. If private property in the means of production actually is an institution that favors one part of society to the detriment of another, then it should be abolished. But if it is found that private property is useful to all, and that human society with its division of labor could not be organized in any other way, then it must be safeguarded so that it can serve its function in the best possible way. We need not here discuss the confusion that must arise about all moral concepts if law and moral precepts disallow, or at least revile, something that must be preserved as the foundation of social life. And why should anything be prohibited in the expectation that the prohibition will be largely circumvented?

Anyone defending interventionism with such arguments is undoubtedly seriously deluded regarding the extent of the productivity loss caused by government interventions. Surely, the adaptability of the capitalist economy has negated many obstacles placed in the way of entrepreneurial activity. We constantly observe that entrepreneurs are succeeding in supplying the markets with more and better products and services despite all difficulties put in their way by law and administration. But we cannot calculate how much better those products and services would be today, without expenditure of additional labor, if the hustle and bustle of government were not aiming (inadvertently, to be sure) at making things worse. We are thinking of the consequences of all trade restrictions on which there can be no differences of opinion. We are thinking of the obstructions to production improvements through the fight against cartels and trusts. We are thinking of the consequences of price controls. We are thinking of the artificial raising of wage rates through collective coercion, the denial of protection to all those willing to work, unemployment compensation, and, finally, the denial of the freedom to move from country to country, all of which have made the unemployment of millions of workers a permanent phenomenon.

Etatists and socialists are calling the great crisis from which the world economy has been suffering since the end of the World War the crisis of capitalism. In reality, it is the crisis of interventionism.

In a static economy there may be idle land, but no unemployed capital or labor. At the unhampered, market, rate of wages all workers find employment. If, other conditions being equal, somewhere workers are released, for instance, on account of an introduction of new labor-saving processes, wage rates must fall. At the new, lower rates then all workers find employment again. In the capitalist social order unemployment is merely a transition and friction phenomenon. Various conditions that impede the free flow of labor from place to place, from country to country, may render the equalization of wage rates more difficult. They may also lead to differences in compensation of the various types of labor. But with freedom for entrepreneurs and capitalists they could never lead to large-scale and permanent unemployment. Workers seeking employment could always find work by adjusting their wage demands to market conditions.

If the market determination of wage rates had not been disrupted, the effects of the World War and the destructive economic policies of the last decades would have led to a decline in wage rates, but not to unemployment. The scope and duration of unemployment, interpreted today as proof of the failure of capitalism, results from the fact that labor unions and unemployment compensation are keeping wage rates higher than the unhampered market would set them. Without unemployment compensation and the power of labor unions to prevent the competition of nonmembers willing to work, the pressure of supply would soon bring about a wage adjustment that would assure employment to all hands. We may regret the consequences of the antimarket and anticapitalistic policy in recent decades, but we cannot change them. Only reduction in consumption and hard labor can replace the capital that was lost, and only the formation of new capital can raise the marginal productivity of labor and thus wage rates.

Unemployment compensation cannot eradicate the evil. It merely delays the ultimately unavoidable adjustment of wages to the fallen marginal productivity. And since the compensation is usually not paid from income, but out of capital, ever more capital is consumed and future marginal productivity of labor further reduced.

However, we must not assume that an immediate abolition of all the obstacles to the smooth functioning of the capitalist economic order would instantly eradicate the consequences of many decades of intervention. Vast amounts of producers' goods have been destroyed. Trade restrictions and other mercantilistic measures have caused malinvestments of even greater amounts that yield little or nothing. The withdrawal of large fertile areas of the world (e.g., Russia and Siberia) from the international exchange system has led to unproductive readjustments in primary production and processing. Even under the most favorable conditions, many years will pass before the traces of the fallacious policies of the last decades can be erased. But there is no other way to the greater well-being for all.

# 6.
# The Doctrine of Interventionism

To prescientific thinkers, a human society built on private property in the means of production seemed to be naturally chaotic. It received its order, so they thought, only from imposed precepts of morality and law. Society can exist only if buyer and seller observe justice and fairness. Government must intervene in order to avoid the evil that flows from an arbitrary deviation from the "just price." This opinion prevailed in all remarks on social life until the eighteenth century. It appeared for the last time in all its naiveté in the writings of the mercantilists.

The anticapitalist writers are emphasizing that classical economics served the "interests" of the "bourgeoisie," which allegedly explains its own success, and led the bourgeois class to its successes. Surely, no one can doubt that the freedom achieved by classical liberalism paved the way for the incredible development of productive forces during the last century. But it is a sad mistake to believe that by opposing intervention classical liberalism gained acceptance more easily. It faced the opposition of all those whom the feverish activity of government granted protection, favors, and privileges. The fact that classical liberalism nevertheless could prevail was due to its intellectual victory, which checkmated the defenders of privilege. It was not new that the victims of privilege favored their abolition. But it was new that the attack on the system of privilege was so successful, which must be credited exclusively to the intellectual victory of classical liberalism.

Classical liberalism was victorious with economics and through it. No other economic ideology can be reconciled with the science of catallactics. During the 1820s and 1830s, an attempt was made in England to use economics for demonstrating that the capitalist order does not function satisfactorily, and that it is unjust. From this Karl Marx then created his "scientific" socialism. But even if these writers had succeeded in proving their case against capitalism, they would have had to prove further that another social order, like socialism, is better than capitalism. This they were not able to do; they could not even prove that a social order could actually be built on public property in the means of production. By merely rejecting and ostracizing any discussion of the problems of socialism as "utopian" they obviously did not solve anything.

Eighteenth century writers then discovered what had already been published by earlier writers on money and prices. They discovered the science of economics which replaced the collection of moral maxims, the manuals of police regulations, and the aphoristic remarks on their successes and failures. They learned that prices are not set arbitrarily, but are determined within narrow limits by the market situation, and that all practical problems can be accurately analyzed. They recognized that the laws of the market draw entrepreneurs and owners of the means of production into the service of consumers, and that their economic actions do not result from arbitrariness, but from the necessary adjustment to given conditions. These facts alone gave life to a science of economics and a system of catallactics. Where the earlier writers saw only arbitrariness and coincidence, the classical economists saw necessity and regularity. In fact, they substituted science and system for debates on police regulations.

The classical economists were not yet fully aware that the private property order alone offers the foundation for a society based on division of labor, and that the public property system is unworkable. Influenced by mercantilist thought, they contrasted productivity with profitability, which gave rise to the question of whether or not the socialist order is preferable to the capitalist order. But they clearly understood that, except for syndicalism which they did not see, the only alternatives are capitalism and socialism, and that "intervention" in the functioning of the private property order, which is so popular with both people and government, is unsuitable.

The tools of science do not enable us to sit in judgment of the "justice" of a social institution or order. Surely, we may decry this or that as "unjust" or "improper"; but if we cannot substitute anything better for what we condemn, it behooves us to save our words.

But all this does not concern us here. Only this matters for us: no one ever succeeded in demonstrating that, disregarding syndicalism, a third social order is conceivable and possible other than that based on private property in the means or production or that built on public property. The

37

middle system of property that is hampered, guided, and regulated by government is in itself contradictory and illogical. Any attempt to introduce it in earnest must lead to a crisis from which either socialism or capitalism alone can emerge.

This is the irrefutable conclusion of economics. He who undertakes to recommend a third social order of regulated private property must flatly deny the possibility of scientific knowledge in the field of economics. The Historical School in Germany did just that, and the Institutionalists in the U.S. are doing it today. Economics is formally abolished, prohibited, and replaced by state and police science, which registers what government has decreed, and recommends what still is to be decreed. They fully realize that they are harking back to mercantilism, even to the canon doctrine of just price, and are discarding all the work of economics.

The German Historical School and its many followers abroad never thought it necessary to cope with the problems of catallactics. They were completely satisfied with the arguments which Gustav Schmoller presented in the famous *Methodenstreit* and his disciples, e.g., Hasbach, repeated after him. In the decades between the Prussian constitutional conflict (1862) and the Weimar constitution (1919), only three men sensed the problems of social reform: Philippovich, Stolzmann, and Max Weber. Among these three, only Philippovich had any knowledge of the nature and content of theoretical economics. In his system, catallactics and interventionism stand side by side, but no bridge leads from the former to the latter, and there is no attempted solution to the great problem. Stolzmann basically seeks to realize what Schmoller and Brentano had merely suggested. It is a sad commentary, however, that the School's only representative who really attacked the problem was utterly ignorant of what his opposition was saying. And Max Weber, preoccupied with quite different matters, stopped half way, because theoretical economics was alien to him. Perhaps he would have gone further had he not been cut off by early death.

For several decades there has been talk at German universities of a reawakening of an interest in theoretical economics. We may mention a number of authors such as Liefmann, Oppenheimer, Gottl, et cetera, who ardently denounce the system of modern subjective economics, of which they know only the "Austrians." We need not here raise the question of whether or not such attacks are justified. But we would like to point out the interesting effect such attacks have had on the discussion of the feasibility of the system of interventionism. Each one of these writers summarily rejects what has been created by theoretical economics—by the Physiocrats, classical writers, and modern authors. In particular, they depict the work of modern economics, especially of the Austrians, as incredible aberrations of the human mind, whereupon they present their own supposedly original systems of theoretical economics, claiming to remove all doubts and solve all problems. The public, unfortunately, is led to believe that in economics everything is uncertain and problematic, and that economic theory merely consists of the personal opinions of various scholars. The excitement created by these authors in German-speaking countries succeeded in obscuring the fact that there is a science of theoretical economics which, despite differences in detail and especially in terminology, is enjoying a good reputation with all friends of science. And in spite of all the critique and reservations, even these writers basically concurred with the theoretical system in its essential questions. But because this was not understood, they did not see the need for examining interventionism from the point of view of economic knowledge.

In addition there was the effect of the argument on the permissibility of value judgments in science. In the hands of the Historical School, political science had become a doctrine of art for statesmen and politicians. At the universities and in textbooks economic demands were presented and proclaimed as "scientific." "Science" condemned capitalism as immoral and unjust, rejected as "radical" the solutions offered by Marxian socialism, and recommended either state socialism or at times the system of private property with government intervention. Economics was no longer a matter of knowledge and ability, but of good intentions. Especially since the beginning of the second decade of this century, this mix of university teaching and politics became objectionable. The public began to hold the official representatives of science in contempt, because they made it their task to confer the blessings of "science" on the party programs of their friends. And the public would no longer tolerate the nuisance that each political party appealed to its favorite judgment of "science," that is, to a university professor marching in its footsteps. When Max Weber and some of his friends demanded that "science" should renounce value judgments and the universities should not be misused for political and economic propaganda, they met with almost universal agreement.

Among those writers who agreed with Max Weber, or at least did not dare contradict him, were several whose whole record stood in open contradiction to the principle of objectivity, and whose literary efforts were nothing but paraphrases of certain political programs. They interpreted "absence of value judgment" in a peculiar way. Ludwig Pohle and Adolf Weber had touched upon the basic problems of interventionism in their discussions of the wage policies of labor associations. The followers of the labor-union doctrines of Brentano and Webb were unable to raise any pertinent objections. But the new postulate of "value-free science" seemed to rescue them from the embarrassment in which they found themselves. Now they could haughtily reject anything that did not suit them, on grounds that it did not square with the dignity of science to interfere with the squabbling of political parties. In good faith, Max Weber had presented the principle of *Wertfreiheit* for a resumption of scientific inquiries into the problems of social life. Instead, it was used by the Historical-Realistic-Social School as protection from the critique of theoretical economics.

Again and again, perhaps intentionally, some writers refuse to recognize the difference between the analysis of economic problems and the formulation of political postulates. We make no value judgments when, for instance, we

40

investigate the consequences of price controls and conclude that a price ceiling set below that of the unhampered market reduces the quantity offered, other conditions being equal. We make no value judgments when we then conclude that price controls do not achieve what the authorities hoped to achieve, and that they are illogical instruments of policy. A physiologist does not indulge in value judgments when he observes that the consumption of hydrocyanic acid destroys human life and, therefore, is illogical as a "nutritional system." Physiology does not answer the question of whether or not a man wants to nourish or kill, or should do so; it merely determines what builds and what destroys, what the nourisher should do and the killer should do in order to act according to his intentions. When I say that price controls are illogical, I mean to assert that they do not achieve the objective they are usually meant to achieve. Now, a Communist could reply: "I favor price controls just because they prevent the smooth functioning of the market mechanism, because they turn human society into a 'senseless chaos' and all the sooner lead to my ideal of communism." Then, the theory of price controls cannot answer him, as physiology cannot answer the man who wants to kill with hydrocyanic acid. We do not resort to value judgments when we demonstrate, in similar fashion, the illogicality of syndicalism and the unrealizability of socialism.

We destroy economics if all its investigations are rejected as inadmissible. We can observe today how many young minds, who under other circumstances would have turned to economic problems, spend themselves on research that does not suit their talents and, therefore, adds little to science. Enmeshed in the errors described above, they shun significant scientific tasks.

# 7.
# The Historical and Practical Arguments for Interventionism

Put on the spot by economic criticism, the representatives of the Historical-Realistic School finally appeal to the "facts." It cannot be denied, they assert, that all the theoretically unsuitable interventions were actually made, and continue to be made. We cannot believe, they contend, that economic practice did not notice this alleged unsuitability. But interventionist norms survived for hundreds of years, and since the decline of liberalism, the world is ruled again by interventionism. All this is said to be sufficient proof that the system is realizable and successful, and not at all illogical. The rich literature of the Historical-Realistic School on the history of economic policies is said to confirm the doctrines of interventionism.[8]

The fact that measures have been taken, and continue to be taken, does not prove that they are suitable. It only proves that their sponsors did not recognize their unsuitability. In fact, contrary to the beliefs of the "empirics," it is not so easy to comprehend the significance of an economic measure. We cannot understand its significance without an insight into the workings of the whole economy, that is, without a comprehensive theory. The authors of works on economic history, economic descriptions, economic policies, and economic statistics usually proceed much too thoughtlessly. Without the necessary theoretical knowledge they engage in tasks for which they are completely unprepared. Whatever the authors of the source material did not

---

8. Zwiedineck-Südenhorst, "Macht oder ökonomisches Gesetz" [Control or economic law], Schmoller's *Yearbook*, 49th year, p. 278 *et seq.*

discover usually escapes the historians' attention also. In a discussion of an economic regulation they are rarely inclined to examine properly and carefully whether the intended result was actually achieved, and if it was achieved, whether it was brought about by the regulation or some other factors. They surely lack the ability to perceive all concomitant effects that, from the point of view of the regulators, were desirable or undesirable. Only in monetary history did the better quality of some works stand out. Their authors were equipped with some knowledge of monetary theory (Gresham's law, quantity theory), and therefore better understood the work they were to do.

The most important qualification of a researcher into "facts" is complete mastery of economic theory. He must interpret the available material in the light of theory. If he does not succeed in this, or it leaves him unsatisfied, he must precisely elaborate the critical point, and formulate the problem that needs to be solved theoretically. Others then may try to solve the task. The failure is his, not that of theory. A theory explains everything. Theories do not fail in individual problems; they fail because of their own shortcomings. He who seeks to replace one theory with another must either fit it into the given system, or create a new system into which it fits. It is wholly unscientific to start with observed "facts" and then announce the failure of "theory" and system. The genius who advances science with new knowledge can gain valuable information from the observation of a minute process, either overlooked or deemed insignificant by those before him. His mind is excited over every object. But the inventor replaces the old with the new, not through negation, but with a view toward the whole and the system.

We need not here deal with the deeper epistemological question of conflicting systems. Nor need we discuss a multiplicity of opposing systems. To investigate the problems of interventionism there are, on the one hand, modern economics together with classical theory and, on the other hand, the deniers of system and theory, no matter how carefully they word their denial of the possibility of theoretical knowledge. Our answer to them is simple: try to create a system of theoretical knowledge that pleases you more than ours. Then we can talk again.

Of course, all the objections raised against theoretical economics are economic "theories." In fact, the objectors themselves are now writing "economic theories" and giving lectures on "theoretical economics." But their work is inadequate because they neglect to weave the individual tenets of their "theory" into a system, a comprehensive theory of catallactics. A theoretical tenet becomes a theory only through a system and in a system. It is very easy to discourse on wage, rent, and interest. But we may speak of a theory only where individual statements are linked to a comprehensive explanation of all market phenomena.

In their experiments the natural sciences can eliminate all disturbing influences and observe the consequences of the change of one factor, other conditions being equal. If the result of the experiment cannot be fitted satisfactorily into the given system of theory, it may invite an expansion of the system, or even its replacement by a new one. But he who would conclude from the result of one experiment that there can be no theoretical perception would invite ridicule. The social sciences lack the experiment. They can never observe the consequences of one factor, other conditions being unchanged. And yet, the deniers of system and theory dare to conclude from some "fact" that a theory, or even all theory, has been refuted.

What is there to be said about general statements such as these: "Britain's industrial supremacy during the eighteenth and nineteenth centuries was the result of mercantile policies in previous centuries," or "The rise in real wages during the last decades of the nineteenth century and the early decades of the twentieth century must be credited to labor unions," or "Land speculation raises rents." Such statements are believed to be drawn directly from experience. This is not gray theory, they tell us, but fruit from the green tree of life. But they adamantly refuse to listen to a theorist who proposes to examine the various tenets of "practical experience" by thinking them through, and wanting to unite them into a systematic structure.

44

All the arguments the Empirical-Realistic School could advance do not replace the lack of a comprehensive theoretical system.

# 8.
# Recent Writings on the Problems of Interventionism

In Germany, the classical country of interventionism, the need to deal seriously with an economic critique of interventionism was scarcely felt. Interventionism came to power without a fight. It could ignore the science of economics created by Englishmen and Frenchmen. Friedrich List denounced it as being injurious to the interests of the German people. Among the few German economists, Thünen was scarcely known, Gossen completely unknown, and Hermann and Mangold without much influence. Menger was "eliminated" in the *Methodenstreit*. Formal science in Germany did not concern itself with economic achievements after the 1870s. All objections were brushed aside by branding them special interest statements of entrepreneurs and capitalists.[9]

In the United States, which now seems to assume leadership in interventionism, the situation is quite different. In the country of J. B. Clark, Taussig, Fetter, Davenport, Young, and Seligman, it is impossible to ignore all the achievements of economics. It was to be expected, therefore,

---

9. See the relevant description of this method by Pohle, *Die gegenwärtige Krisis in der deutschen Volkswirtschaftslehre* [The present crisis in German economics], 2nd ed., Leipzig, 1921, p. 115 *et seq.*

that an attempt would here be made to prove the realizability and suitability of interventionism. John Maurice Clark, formerly a University of Chicago professor and now, as was his great father John Bates Clark, professor at Columbia University in New York City, has undertaken this very task.[10]

We regret, however, that only a single chapter with a few pages deals with the fundamental problems of interventionism. Professor Clark distinguishes between two types of social regulation of economic actions: regulation of incidental matters, "those in which the state is dealing with matters which are incidental to the main transaction," and regulation of essential matters, "those in which the 'heart of the contract' is at stake and the state presumes to fix the terms of the exchange and dictate the consideration in money or in goods, or to say that the exchange shall not take place at all."[11] This distinction roughly coincides with our distinction between production and price intervention. It is clear that an economic consideration of the system of interventionism cannot proceed any differently.

In his analysis of "control of matters incidental to the contract" J. M. Clark does not arrive at any conclusion other than ours in an analysis of production intervention. He too must conclude that "such regulations impose some burdens on industry."[12] This is all that interests us in his discussion. His examination of the political pros and cons of such intervention is irrelevant for our problem.

In his discussion of control of the "heart of the contract," which roughly corresponds to price intervention, Clark first mentions the American control of interest rates. It is circumvented, he asserts, through additional incidental charges that raise the nominal rate to the borrower. An illegal commerce has developed in small loans to consumers. Inasmuch as decent people do not engage in such transactions, they

---

10. J. M. Clark, *Social Control of Business,* (Chicago: University of Chicago Press, 1926).

11. *Ibid.*, p. 450. To avoid any misunderstanding I would like to emphasize that this distinction has nothing to do with the public-law distinction between *essentialia, naturalia,* and *accidentalia negotii* (the indispensably necessary, natural resources, and contract matters).

12. *Ibid.*, p. 451.

are the sphere for unscrupulous operators. As such transactions must shun the light of publicity, exorbitant interest rates are demanded and granted, which exceed by far the rates that would prevail if no rates were fixed. "Charges equivalent to several hundred per cent per year are the common thing. The law multiplies the evil of extortion tenfold." [13]

Nevertheless, Professor Clark does not believe that rate fixing is illogical. In general, the loan market even for this category of consumer loans is to be left free, with a law to prohibit an interest rate higher than the market rate. "The law . . . may render a great service in preventing the exaction of charges which are materially above the true market rate." Therefore, the simplest method, according to Clark, is "to fix a legal rate for this class of loans which liberally covers all costs and necessary inducements, and to forbid all charges in excess of this rate." [14]

Surely, when the interest regulation sanctions the market rates or even exceeds them, it can do no harm. It is useless and superfluous. But if it fixes a rate that is lower than that which would develop in an unhampered market, then all the consequences described so well by Clark must emerge. Why, then, the rate fixing? Clark's answer: it is necessary to avoid unfair discrimination. [15]

The concept of "unfair" or "undue discriminations" originates in the field of monopoly. [16] If the monopolist as seller is in the position to classify the potential buyers according to purchasing power and desire intensity, to whom he offers his commodity or service at different prices, then he does better without a uniform price. Such conditions are given in most cases of means of transportation, electric power plants, and similar enterprises. The freight rates of railroads represent a nearly classical case of such a differentiation. But

---

13. *Ibid.*, p. 453 *et seq.*
14. *Ibid.*, p. 454.
15. *Ibid.*
16. See the voluminous American literature: Nash, *The Economics of Public Utilities*, New York, 1925, p. 97, 371; Wherry, *Public Utilities and the Law*, New York, 1925, pp. 3 *et seq.*, 82 *et seq.*, 174. See also Clark, *op. cit.*, p. 398 *et seq.*

without further explanation one cannot call this practice "unjust," an interventionist charge so naively and resentfully made against monopolists. However, we need not be concerned with the ethical justification of intervention. From a scientific point of view, we merely must observe that there is room for government intervention in the case of monopoly.

But there is also a differential treatment of the various classes of buyers that runs counter to the interests of monopolies. This may be the case where the monopoly is managed as a part of a larger enterprise in which the monopoly serves objectives other than greatest profitability. Let us disregard all cases in which the monopolist either is a compulsory association or acts under its influence, seeking to achieve certain national, military, or social objectives. Freight rates, for instance, may be set to accommodate foreign trade, or municipal services may be priced according to customers' income. In all such cases the interventionists approve of the differentiation. To us, only those cases are significant in which the monopolist resorts to differentiation that runs counter to his profit interests. It may be that he takes into consideration the interests of his other enterprises that are more important to him. Or he wants to disadvantage a buyer for personal reasons, or force him to do or not to do something. In the United States, railroads have favored individual shippers through concessions of lower freight rates, which often forced their competitors to close their businesses or sell them at depressed prices. The public generally censured such practices because they promoted industrial concentration and formation of monopolies. Public opinion viewed the disappearance of competition in individual industries with great alarm. It failed to recognize that competition takes place among producers and sellers not only within each individual branch of production, but also between all related goods, and in the final analysis, between all economic goods. And it did not recognize that the monopolistic price charged by the few genuine monopolies—mining and similar primary production—is not so detrimental to all, as the naive foes of monopolies are willing to assume.[17]

But there is no talk of monopoly in Clark's case of the loan market for consumers, small farmers, merchants and tradesmen. How is it possible to practice unfair discrimination? When one lender does not lend at the market rate the borrower may simply go to another. Of course, it cannot be denied that everyone is inclined—especially among the borrowers of this lowest category—to overestimate his own credit rating, and call the rates demanded by creditors too high.

J. M. Clark proceeds from a discussion of interest regulation to that of minimum wages. "Artificial" wage boosts, he believes, lead to unemployment. The rise in wages raises production costs, and thus the product price. The quantity that was sold at the lower price can no longer be marketed at this higher price. On the one hand, this leaves unsatisfied buyers who would like to buy at the no longer quoted lower price, and on the other hand, it causes unemployment of workers who are willing to work at lower wage rates. Finally, entrepreneurs will be willing to bring this potential demand and supply together.

So far we can again agree with Clark. But then comes an assertion that completely misses the mark—that is, that "the regulations affecting the incidental conditions of employment" must have the same consequences since they too raise production costs.[18] But this is not correct. If wages are freely determined in the labor market, no raise in wages above the market rate can occur as a result of interventions, such as the shortening of labor time, mandatory insurance of workers at the expense of employers, regulations of workshop conditions, vacations of workers with full pay, et cetera. All these costs are shifted to wages and are borne by

---

17. See my *Gemeinwirtschaft*, Jena, 1922, p. 382 *et seq.* [English-language edition: *Socialism* (London: Jonathan Cape, 1936), p. 391 *et seq.*], also my *Liberalismus*, Jena, 1927, p. 80 *et seq.* [English-language edition: *The Free and Prosperous Commonwealth* (New York: D. Van Nostrand Co., Inc., 1962), p. 92 *et seq.*].

18. Clark, *op. cit.*, p. 455.

the workers. This fact could be overlooked because such social interventions were introduced mainly at a time when real wages were rising and the purchasing power of money was falling. Thus, net wages paid to workers continued to rise in terms of both money and purchasing power despite the ever-rising social costs placed on the employer. His calculations include not only the workers' wages, but also all costs resulting from their employment.

Clark's further remarks have no bearing on our problem. He believes that wage increases, like other interventions on behalf of workers, "may prove self-sustaining through raising the level of personal efficiency, through furnishing an added stimulus to the employer's search for improved methods, and through hastening the elimination of the least efficient employers and transfering their business to those who will conduct it more efficiently." [19] All this can also be said about an earthquake or any other natural catastrophe.

Professor Clark is trained too well in theory and is too perceptive not to notice how untenable his reasoning actually is. He concludes, therefore, that the question of whether or not a given intervention is a "violation of economic law" is basically "a question of degree." In the final analysis, Clark assures us, we must consider how severely the intervention affects production costs or market prices. The law of supply and demand is "no thing of precision and inexorable rigidity." Many times "a small change in costs of production" has no effect at all on final prices—when, for instance, the price is usually quoted in round numbers and the merchants absorb small changes in costs or wholesale prices. Clark's final word: "A large increase in wage rates may be a 'violation of economic law,' in the sense in which we are using the term, where a small increase would not be." [20]

Upon careful reflection, Professor Clark yields to all the objections by those writers who call interventionism unsuitable and illogical. It is obvious and undeniable that the quantitative consequences of an intervention depend on the

---

19. *Ibid.*
20. *Ibid.*

severity of the intervention. A small earthquake destroys less than a big one, and a very small earthquake may leave no visible traces at all.

It is utterly irrelevant that Clark nevertheless clings to the statement that such interventions can be made and advocated. He must admit that this leads to further measures in order to alleviate the consequences. For instance, when price controls are imposed, there must be a rationing in order to remove the discrepancy between supply and demand. And it will be necessary to stimulate production directly because the normal impetus will be lost.[21] At this point Clark unfortunately discontinues his discussion. Had he proceeded he would necessarily have come to the conclusion that there are only two alternatives: either to abstain from all intervention, or, if this is not the intention, to add ever new interventions in order to eliminate "the discrepancy between supply and demand which the public policy has created," until all production and distribution are controlled by the social apparatus of coercion, that is, until the means of production are nationalized.

In the case of minimum wage legislation it is a very unsatisfactory solution for Professor Clark to recommend that the workers who lost their jobs be employed in public works.[22] And when he points at "energy, intelligence and loyalty" calling for government intervention, he merely reveals his embarrassment.[23]

In his second to last sentence of this chapter dealing with fundamentals, Clark concludes that "government can do a great deal of good by merely seeing to it that everyone gets the benefit of the market rate, whatever that is, and thus prevent the ignorant from being exploited on account of their ignorance."[24] This concurs completely with the position of classical liberalism: government shall be limited to the protection of private property and the elimination of all obstacles to free market access for individuals or groups of

21. *Ibid.*, p. 456.
22. *Ibid.*
23. *Ibid.*, p. 457.
24. *Ibid.*, p. 459.

individuals. This is nothing but another wording of the principle: *laissez faire, laissez passer*. It is insignificant that Professor Clark apparently believes that a special information program is necessary for the attainment of this objective. Ignorance of the market situation alone cannot prevent potential buyers or workers from exploring the situation. If the sellers and entrepreneurs are not hampered in searching for customers and workers, their competition will reduce goods prices and raise wages until the market rate is attained. But whatever it be, classical liberal principles are not violated if government undertakes to publish relevant data on the formation of market prices.

The result of Clark's inquiry into our problem thus does not contradict our own analysis earlier in this essay. Despite Clark's eagerness to prove that the popular interventions are not unsuitable and illogical, he did not succeed in adding anything but the observation that the consequences are insignificant if the intervention is quantitatively unimportant, and that important interventions have undesirable consequences that need to be alleviated through more intervention. At this point Clark unfortunately halted his discussion. If he had proceeded to its conclusion, which he should have done, it too would have clearly revealed the only alternative: either private property in the means of production is permitted to function freely, or control over the means of production is transferred to organized society, to its apparatus of coercion, the state. It would have revealed that there can be no other alternative but socialism or capitalism.

Thus, Clark's work also, which is the most complete expression of American interventionism, can come to no other conclusion in its discussion of the basic questions of interventionism. Interventionism is a system that is contradictory and unsuitable even from the point of view of its sponsors, that cannot be carried out logically, and whose introduction in every case can effect nothing but disturbances in the smooth functioning of the social order based on private property.

We owe the most recent German discussion of our problem to Richard Strigl, a member of the Austrian School. Although not so outspoken as J. M. Clark, he too sympathizes with interventionism. Every line of his work, which seeks to analyze theoretically the wage problems of interventionism,[25] clearly reflects his desire to acclaim as much as possible social policy in general and labor union policies in particular. All Strigl's statements are carefully worded in the same manner that authors of previous centuries worded theirs in order to escape inquisition or censure.[26] But all the concessions which his heart grants to interventionistic thinking concern only secondary matters and the formulation of doctrine. Regarding the problem itself, Strigl's perceptive analysis comes to no conclusion other than that drawn in scientific economic analysis. The gist of his doctrine is visible in the sentence: "The greater the service a worker can render, the more he will earn, provided his service is useful in the economy; it does not matter whether his wage is determined in the free market or agreed upon by collective contract."[27] It obviously grieves him that this is so, but he cannot and will not deny it.

Strigl emphasizes that artificial wage increases create unemployment.[28] This is undoubtedly the case where wages are raised in individual industries only, or in individual countries only, or where they are raised unevenly in different industries and countries, or where monetary policies are used to stem a general rise in prices. Undoubtedly Strigl's case is important for an understanding of present-day conditions. For a thorough understanding of the problem, however, we must rely upon another basic assumption. To have universal validity our analysis must assume that the rise in wages occurs evenly and simultaneously in different industries and countries, and that monetary factors do not intervene. Only then can we completely understand interventionism.

---

25. See Strigl, *Angewandte Lohntheorie. Untersuchungen über die wirtschaftlichen Grundlagen der Socialpolitik* [Applied wage theory. Inquiries into the economic foundations of social policy], Leipzig and Vienna, 1926.
26. *Ibid.*, especially p. 71 *et seq.*
27. *Ibid.*, p. 106.
28. *Ibid.*, p. 63 *et seq.*, p. 116 *et seq.*

Of all the interventionist measures none is probably under stronger attack in Germany and Austria than the eight-hour workday. Many believe that the economic emergency can be met only be repealing the eight-hour law: more work and more intensive work are needed. It is taken for granted that the lengthening of labor time and the improvement in labor efficiency would not be accompanied by higher wages, or at least that the increases would trail the rising labor efficiency, so that labor would become less expensive. Simultaneously, a reduction in all kinds of "social costs" is demanded, such as the elimination of the "welfare tax" payable by the businessman in Austria. It is tacitly assumed that he would retain the savings from such cost reductions, and that his labor costs would thus be reduced indirectly. Efforts to reduce wages directly are insignificant at the present time.

In social journals and economic literature, the discussion of the problems of the eight-hour day, and the intensity of labor reveals a slow but steady progress in economic understanding. Even writers who do not hide their bias for interventionism, admit the cogency of the most important arguments against interventionism. Seldom do we still meet the blindness in a fundamental understanding of such matters that characterized our literature before the war.

Surely, the supremacy of the interventionist school has not yet been overthrown. Of Schmoller's state socialism and etatism and of Marx's egalitarian socialism and communism only the names have survived in political life; the socialist ideal itself has ceased to exert a direct political effect. Its followers, even those who were willing to shed blood to bring it about a few years ago, have now postponed it or given up entirely. But interventionism as Schmoller and Marx advocated it—Schmoller, as a foe of all "theory," quite unhesitatingly; Marx with bad conscience about its insoluble contradiction to all his theories—now dominates the climate of opinion.

We need not examine here whether the political conditions are ripe for the German people and other leading nations to turn away from interventionistic policies. An impartial analysis of the state of affairs may show that interventionism continues to advance. This can hardly be denied for Great Britain and the United States. But surely it is as futile today as it was in the past to defend interventionism as meaningful and purposeful from the point of view of economic theory. In fact, it is neither meaningful nor purposeful from any point of view. There is no road from economics to interventionism. All interventionistic successes in practical politics were "victories over economics."

# THE HAMPERED MARKET ECONOMY

## 1.
## The Prevailing Doctrine of the Hampered Market Economy

With a few exceptions contemporary commentators on economic problems are advocating economic intervention. This unanimity does not necessarily mean that they approve of interventionistic measures by government or other coercive powers. Authors of economics books, essays, articles, and political platforms demand interventionistic measures before they are taken, but once they have been imposed no one likes them. Then everyone—usually even the authorities responsible for them—call them insufficient and unsatisfactory. Generally the demand then arises for the replacement of unsatisfactory interventions by other, more suitable measures. And once the new demands have been met, the same scenario begins all over again. The universal desire for the interventionist system is matched by the rejection of all concrete measures of the interventionist policy.

57

Sometimes, during discussion of a partial or complete repeal of a regulation, there are voices against changing it, but they rarely approve the given measure; they wish to prevent even worse measures. For instance, scarcely ever have livestock farmers been pleased with the tariffs and veterinary regulations that were adopted in order to restrict the importation of livestock, meats, and fats from abroad. But as soon as consumers demand the repeal or relaxation of these restrictions, the farmers rise in their defense. The champions of legislative labor protection have labeled every regulation adopted so far as unsatisfactory—at best to be accepted as an installment on what needs to be done. But if one such regulation faces repeal—for instance, the legal limitation of the workday to eight hours—they rise in its defense.

This attitude toward specific interventions is readily understood by anyone who recognizes that intervention necessarily is illogical and unsuitable, as it can never attain what its champions and authors hope to attain. It is remarkable, however, that it is obstinately defended in spite of its shortcomings, and in spite of the failure of all attempts at demonstrating its theoretical logic. To most observers, the thought of returning to classical liberal policies appears so absurd that they rarely bother to give it thought.

The defenders of interventionism often appeal to the notion that classical liberalism belongs to a past era. Today, they tell us, we are living in the age of "constructive economic policy," namely, interventionism. The wheel of history cannot be turned back, and that which has vanished cannot be restored. He who calls for classical liberalism and thus proclaims the solution as "back to Adam Smith" is demanding the impossible.

It is not at all true that contemporary liberalism is identical with the British liberalism of the eighteenth and nineteenth centuries. Certainly modern liberalism is built on the great ideas developed by Hume, Adam Smith, Ricardo, Bentham, and Wilhelm Humboldt. But liberalism is no closed doctrine and rigid dogma. It is an application of the principles of science to man's social life, to politics. Economics and social science have made great strides since the beginning of liberal doctrine, and thus liberalism also had to change, although the basic thought remained unaltered. He who makes the effort to study modern liberalism will soon discover the differences between the two. He will learn that knowledge of liberalism cannot be derived from Adam Smith alone, and that the demand for repeal of interventionistic measures is not identical with the call, Return to Adam Smith.

Modern liberalism differs from the liberalism of the eighteenth and nineteenth centuries at least as much as modern interventionism differs from the mercantilism of the seventeenth and eighteenth centuries. It is illogical to call the return to free trade an anachronism if the return to the system of protection and prohibition is not also seen as an anachronism.

Writers who credit the change in economic policy simply to the spirit of the age surely expect very little from a scientific explanation of interventionism. The capitalist spirit is said to have been replaced by the spirit of the hampered economy. Capitalism has grown old and, therefore, must yield to the new. And this new is said to be the economy that is hampered by government and other intervention. Anyone who seriously believes that such statements can refute the conclusions of economics regarding the effects of import duties and price controls truly cannot be helped.

Another popular doctrine works with the mistaken concept of "free competition." At first, some writers create an ideal of competition that is free and equal in conditions— like the postulates of natural science—and then they find that the private property order does not at all correspond to this ideal. But because realization of this postulate of "competition that is really free and equal in conditions" is believed to be the highest objective of economic policy, they suggest various reforms. In the name of the ideal, some are demanding a kind of socialism they call "liberal" because they apparently perceive the essence of liberalism in this ideal. And others are demanding various other interventionistic measures. But the economy is no prize contest in which the participants compete under the conditions of the rules of the game. If it is to be determined which horse can run a certain distance in the shortest period of time, the conditions should be equal for all horses. However, are we to treat the economy like an efficiency test to determine which applicant under equal conditions can produce at lowest costs?

Competition as a social phenomenon has nothing in common with competition in play. It is a terminological confusion to transfer the postulate of "equal conditions" from the rules of sport or from the arrangement of scientific and technological experiments to economic policy. In society, not only in the capitalist order, but in every conceivable social order, there is competition among individuals. The sociologists and economists of the eighteenth and nineteenth centuries demonstrated how competition works in the social order that rests on private property in the means of production. This was an essential part of their critique of the interventionistic policies of the mercantilistic police and welfare state. Their investigations revealed how illogical and unsuitable interventionistic measures were. Pressing further they also learned that the economic order that corresponds best to man's economic goals is that built on private property. Surely the mercantilists wondered how the people would be provided for if government left them alone. The classical liberals answered that the competition of businessmen will supply the markets with the economic goods needed by consumers. In general they couched their demand for elimination of intervention in these words: the freedom of competition must not be limited. With the slogan of "free competition" they demanded that the social function of private property not be hampered by government intervention. Thus the misunderstanding could arise that the essence of liberal programs was not private property, but "free competition." Social critics began to chase a nebulous phantom, "genuinely free competition," which was nothing more than a creature of an insufficient study of the problem and occupation with catchwords.[1]

---

1. See the critique of such errors, Halm, *Die Konkurrenz* [Competition], Munich and Leipzig, 1929, especially p. 131 *et seq.*

The apology for interventionism and the refutation of the critique of interventions by economic theory are taken much too lightly with the assertion, e.g., by Lampe, that this critique

> is justified only when it is shown simultaneously that the existing economic order corresponds to the ideal of free competition. Only under this condition must every government intervention be tantamount to a reduction in economic productivity. But no serious social scientist would venture today to speak of such a pre-established economic harmony, as the classical economists and their optimistic-liberal epigones envisage it. There are tendencies in the market mechanism that bring about an adjustment of disrupted economic relations. But these forces prevail only "in the long run," while the readjustment process is interrupted by more or less sharp frictions. This gives rise to situations in which intervention by "social power" not only can be necessary politically, but also suitable economically . . . provided expert advice on the basis of strictly scientific analysis is available to the public power and that it is followed.[2]

It is most remarkable that this thesis was not written during the 1870s or 1880s when the Socialists of the Chair untiringly offered to the high authorities their infallible remedies for the social problem and their promises for the dawn of glorious times. But it was written in 1927. Lampe still does not see that the scientific critique of interventionism has nothing to do with an "ideal of free competition" and "pre-established harmony."[3] He who scientifically analyzes interventionism does not maintain that the unhampered economy is in any sense ideal, good, or free from frictions. He does not contend that every intervention is tantamount to a "reduction in economic productivity." His critique merely

---

2. Lampe, *Notstandarbeiten oder Lohnabbau?* [Public works or wage reductions?], Jena, 1927, p. 104 *et seq.*
3. On "pre-established harmony" see further my essay below, "Anti-Marxism."

demonstrates that interventions cannot achieve the objectives which their authors and promoters want to achieve, and that they must have consequences which even their authors and sponsors did not want and which run counter to their own intentions. This is what the apologists of interventionism must answer. But they are without an answer.

Lampe presents a program of "productive interventionism" consisting of three points.[4] The first point is that the public authority "must possibly stand for a slow reduction of the wage level." At least Lampe does not deny that any "public authority" attempt at holding wage rates above those an unhampered market would establish must create unemployment. But he overlooked the fact that his own proposal would bring about, to a lesser degree and for a limited time, the intervention which he himself knew to be unsuitable. When compared with such vague and incomplete proposals, the advocates of all-round controls have the advantage of seeming logical. Lampe reproaches me for not caring how long the transitional frictional unemployment will last and how severe it may be.[5] Now, without intervention it neither will last long nor affect many. But undoubtedly the enactment of Lampe's proposal can only bring about its prolonged duration and its aggravated severity. Even Lampe cannot deny this in the light of his other discussion.

Anyway, we must bear in mind that a critique of interventionism does not ignore the fact that when some production interventions are eliminated special frictions are generated. If, for instance, all import restrictions were lifted today, the greatest difficulties would be evident for a short time, but there would soon be an unprecedented rise in the productivity of human labor. These inevitable frictions cannot be mitigated through an orderly lengthening of the time taken for such a reduction of the protection, nor are they always aggravated by such a lengthening. However, in the case of government interferences with prices, a slow and gradual reduction, when compared with their immediate

---

4. Lampe, *op. cit.*, p. 127 *et seq.*
5. *Ibid.*, p. 105.

abolition, only prolongs the time during which the undesirable consequences of the intervention continue to be felt.

The two other points of Lampe's "productive interventionism" require no special critique. In fact, one of them is not interventionistic, and the other actually aims at its abolition. In the second point of his program, Lampe demands that public authority eliminate the numerous institutional obstacles that stifle the occupational and regional mobility of labor. But this means elimination of all those government and labor union measures that impede mobility. This is basically the old demand of *laissez passer*, the very opposite of interventionism. And in his third point, Lampe demands that the central political authority gain "an early and dependable overview of the whole economic situation," which surely is no intervention. An overview of the economic situation can be useful to everybody, even to government, if the conclusion is reached that there should be no interference at all.

When we compare Lampe's interventionistic program with others of a few years ago, we recognize how much more modest the claims of this school have become. This is progress of which the critics of interventionism can be proud.

# 2.
# The Thesis of Schmalenbach

Considering the dismal intellectual poverty and sterility of nearly all books and papers defending interventionism, we must take notice of an attempt by Schmalenbach to prove the inevitability of the "hampered economy."

Schmalenbach starts from the assumption that the capital intensity of industry is growing continuously. This leads to the inference that fixed costs become ever more significant while proportional costs lose in significance.

> The fact that an ever larger share of production costs is fixed causes the old era of a free economy to draw to a close, and a new era of a hampered economy to begin. It is a characteristic of proportional costs that they occur with every item produced, with every ton delivered. . . . When prices fall below production costs, production is curtailed with corresponding savings in proportional costs. But if the lion's share of production costs consists of fixed costs, a production cutback does not reduce costs correspondingly. When prices then decline it is rather futile to offset their fall through production cutbacks. It is cheaper to continue production with average costs. Of course, the business now suffers a loss which, however, is smaller than it would be in the case of production cutbacks with nearly undiminished costs. The modern economy with its high fixed costs thus has been deprived of the remedy that automatically coordinates production and consumption, and thereby restores the economic equilibrium. The economy lacks the ability to adjust production to consumption because to a large extent proportional costs have become rigid.[6]

This shifting of production costs within the enterprise "almost alone" is "guiding us from the old economic order to the new one." "The old great era of the nineteenth century, the epoch of free enterprise, was possible only when production costs generally were proportional in nature. It ceased to be possible when the proportion of fixed costs be-

---

6. Schmalenbach, "Die Betriebswirtschaftslehre an der Schwelle der neuen Wirtschaftsverfassung" [The doctrines of business administration at the dawn of a new economic constitution] in *Zeitschrift für Handelswissenschaftliche Forschung* [Journal for trade research], 22nd year, 1928, p. 244 *et seq.*

came ever more significant." Since the growth of fixed costs has not yet stopped and will probably continue for a long time, it is obviously hopeless to count on a return of the free economy.[7]

Schmalenbach at first offers proof for the relative rise in fixed costs with the remark that the continuous growth of enterprise size "is necessarily connected with an expansion, even a relative expansion, of the department that is heading the whole organization."[8] I doubt that. The superiority of a larger enterprise consists, among other things, in managerial costs lower than those of smaller enterprises. The same is true for the commercial departments, especially the sales organizations.

Of course, Schmalenbach is completely correct when he emphasizes that the costs of management and many other general costs cannot be reduced substantially when the enterprise works only at one-half or one-fourth of its capacity. But as management costs decline with the growth of the enterprise, calculated per unit of output, they are less significant in this age of big business and giant enterprises than formerly in the age of smaller operations.

But Schmalenbach's emphasis is not here; it lies on the rise in capital intensity. He believes that he can simply conclude from the continuous formation of new capital and progressive application of machines and equipment— which is undoubtedly true in a capitalist economy—that the ratio of fixed costs will rise. But he must prove first that this is actually the case for the whole economy, not just for individual enterprises. In fact, continuing capital formation leads to a decline in the marginal productivity of capital and an increase in that of labor. The share that goes to capital declines, and that of labor rises. Schmalenbach did not consider this, which negates the very premise of his thesis.[9]

But let us also ignore this shortcoming and examine Schmalenbach's doctrine itself. Let us raise the question of

---

7. *Ibid.*, p. 242 *et seq.*
8. *Ibid.*, p. 243.
9. See Adolf Weber, *Das Ende des Kapitalismus* [The end of capitalism], Munich, 1929, p. 19.

whether a relative rise in fixed costs can actually precipitate entrepreneurial behavior that deprives the economy of its ability to adjust production to demand.

Let us look at an enterprise that either from the start or because of a changed situation does not come up to its earlier expectations. When it was built its founders hoped that the investment capital not only would be amortized and would yield the going rate of interest but, in addition, would pay a profit. Now it has turned out differently. The product price has fallen so much that it covers only a part of production costs—even without allowance for the costs of interest and amortization. A cutback in output cannot bring relief; it cannot make the enterprise profitable. The less it produces, the higher will be the production costs per unit of output and the greater the losses from the sale of each unit (pursuant to our assumption that the fixed costs are very high relative to proportional costs, disregarding even the costs of interest and amortization). There is only one way out of the difficulty: to shut down entirely; only then can further losses be avoided. Of course the situation may not always be so simple. There is hope, perhaps, that the product price will rise again. In the meantime, production is continued because the disadvantages of the shutdown are thought to be greater than the operating losses during the bad time. Until recently most unprofitable railroads were in this situation because automobiles and airplanes entered the competition. They counted upon an increase in traffic, hoping to earn profits some day. But if such special conditions do not exist, production is shut down. Enterprises laboring under less favorable conditions disappear, which establishes the equilibrium between production and demand.

Schmalenbach's error lies in his belief that the cutback in production, necessitated by the decline in prices, must take place through a proportionate cutback of all existing operations. He forgets that there is yet another way, namely, the complete shutdown of all plants working under unfavorable conditions because they can no longer stand the competition of plants producing at lower costs. This is true especially in industries producing raw materials and staples. In finishing industries, where individual plants usually manufacture various items for which production and market conditions may vary, a cutback may be ordered, limiting output to the more profitable items.

This is the situation in a free economy unhampered by government intervention. Therefore, it is utterly erroneous to maintain that a rise in fixed costs denies our economy the ability to adjust production to demand.

It is true that if government interferes with this adjustment process through the imposition of protective tariffs of appropriate size a new possibility arises for producers: they can form a cartel in order to reap monopolistic gains through reductions in output. Obviously, the formation of cartels does not result from some development in the free economy, but is rather the consequence of the government intervention, i.e., the tariff. In the case of coal and brick, the transportation costs, which are so high relative to product value, may, under certain conditions and without government intervention, lead to the formation of cartels with limited local effectiveness. A few metals are found in so few places that even in a free economy the producers may attempt to form a world cartel. But it cannot be said too often that all other cartels owe their existence not to a tendency in a free economy, but to intervention. International cartels generally can be formed only because important production and consumption areas are sheltered from the world market by tariff barriers.

The formation of cartels has nothing to do with the ratio of fixed to proportional costs. The fact that the cartel formation in the finishing industries is proceeding more slowly than in staple industries is not due to the slower rise in fixed costs, as Schmalenbach believes, but to the complex manufacture of goods nearer to consumption, which is too intricate for cartel agreements. Furthermore, it is due to the dispersal of production over numerous enterprises that are more vulnerable to competition by outsiders.

The fixed costs, according to Schmalenbach, prod an enterprise to embark upon expansion in spite of lacking demand. There are facilities in each plant that are used very little; even at full plant operation they are working with degressive costs. To utilize these facilities better the plant is enlarged. "Thus whole industries are expanding their capacities without justification by a rise in demand."[10] We readily admit that this is the case in contemporary Europe with its interventionistic policies, and especially in highly interventionistic Germany. Production is expanded without consideration of the market, but rather in view of the redistribution of cartel quotas and similar considerations. Again, this is a consequence of interventionism, not a factor giving rise to it.

Even Schmalenbach, whose thinking is oriented economically in contrast to that of other observers, could not escape the error that generally characterizes German economic literature. It is erroneous to view developments in Europe, and particularly in Germany under the influence of highly protective tariffs, as the result of free market forces. It cannot be emphasized too often and too emphatically that the German iron, coal, and potash industries are operating under the impact of tariff protection, and, in the case of coal and potash, also under other government intervention, and these are forcing the formation of syndicates. Therefore, to draw conclusions for the free economy from what is happening in those industries is completely incorrect. The "permanent inefficiency" so sharply criticized by Schmalenbach,[11] is no inefficiency of the free economy, but inefficiency of the hampered economy. The "new economic order" is the product of interventionism.

Schmalenbach is convinced that in the not-too-distant future we must reach a state of affairs in which the monopolistic organizations will receive their monopolistic power from the state, and the state will superintend "the performance of the duties incumbent on the monopoly."[12] Surely, if for any reason we reject the return to a free economy, this con-

---

10. Schmalenbach, *op. cit.*, p. 245.
11. *Ibid.*, p. 247.
12. *Ibid.*, p. 249 *et seq.*

clusion completely agrees with that to which every economic analysis of the problems of interventionism must lead. Interventionism as an economic system is unsuitable and illogical. Once this is recognized it leaves us with the choice between lifting all restrictions, or expanding them to a system in which government directs all business decisions —in which the state determines what to produce and how, under what conditions, and to whom the products must be sold. This is a system of socialism in which private property at best survives in name only.

A discussion of the economy of a socialistic community does not belong with this analysis. I have dealt with it in another place.[13]

13. See Mises, *Die Gemeinwirtschaft*, Jena, 1922, p. 94 *et seq*. [English-language edition: *Socialism* (London: Jonathan Cape, 1936), p. 111 *et seq*.]

# SOCIAL LIBERALISM[1]

# 1.
# Introduction

Heinrich Herkner, president of the Association for Social Policy, recently published his autobiography under the subtitle "The Life of a Socialist of the Chair." In it he made it his task "to facilitate an understanding of the closing era of German academic socialism."[2] In fact, it cannot be denied that the Socialists of the Chair have said everything they meant to say, and it seems their supremacy is now declining. Therefore, it is time for an examination of their achievements.

On the occasion of Gustav Schmoller's seventieth birthday, the most eminent members of the Historical-Realistic School cooperated in a work that was to present the results of the efforts of German economics during the nineteenth century.[3] A summary of the forty monographs of this book was never written. The preface expressly states that it must

---

1. *Zeitschrift für die Gesamte Staatswissenschaft* [Journal for all the social sciences], vol. 81, 1926.

2. *Volkswirtschaftslehre der Gegenwart in Selbstdarstellung* [Contemporary economics in an autobiography], edited by Dr. Felix Meiner, vol. I, Leipzig, 1924, p. 113.

3. *Die Entwicklung der deutschen Volkswirtschaftslehre im 19. Jahrhundert* [The development of German economics during the ninteenth century], Leipzig, 1908, two volumes.

be left to a future analysis to take stock of the nature and extent of the progress of German economic science as a whole.[4]

If anyone had tried to write this analysis, it undoubtedly would have been disappointing. The summary more than the individual monographs would have revealed how few of its goals the School did achieve. It would have shown how the School, whenever it touched upon fundamental questions, could not escape borrowing from the discoveries of a theoretical school that is quite low in its esteem. In each contribution that merely half-way meets its requirements, the work of economic theorists is clearly visible despite the fact that they stood apart from the School and were attacked by it. Bernhard's contribution on wages, for instance, arrives at the conclusion that "the Historical-Statistical School barely touched the main problem of wages." It merely launched detailed investigations, but on the great questions it "finally could stutter only the confession: the processes are more complicated than the sum of our detailed investigations. There would be no new German research if it were not for the so-called abstract Austrian School."[5] If this is true of wages, a topic on which the Socialists of the Chair loved to expound, how much more must it apply to all other problems!

We are gaining the same impression from all other collections of essays this School has published. In *Outlines of Social Economics* Austrian economists dealt with the history of thought and with economic theory. And the classical contributions by Menger, Böhm-Bawerk, Wieser, and a few other "theorists" are the only essays of lasting interest in the ten-thousand-page collection of the third edition of the *Handbook of Social Sciences*.

There is yet another comprehensive *Festschrift* that seeks to present the entire science in monographs. But there are signs that such collections covering motley problems, torturing readers and embarrassing librarians, are gradually being replaced with collections dealing with one set of prob-

---

4. *Ibid.*, vol. I, p. viii.
5. Bernhard, "Der Arbeitslohn" [Wages] in *ibid.*, vol. I, XI, p. 11 *et seq.*

lems only. On the occasion of the eightieth birthday of Lujo Brentano, the veteran dean of academic socialism in and outside Germany, his students published *Economics After the War.*[6]

Naturally, the quality of the individual contributions varies greatly. And it need not be emphasized that the twenty-nine contributors worked independently and took no notice of each other's theories and ideologies. But a common thread appears throughout the works—especially those the editors thought most important and which Brentano probably read with greatest delight—namely, the intention to defend and elaborate the "Brentano system." The external conditions for such a task are less favorable today than seventeen years ago. When the Schmoller *Festschrift* appeared, academic socialism and Historical-Realistic economics stood at the zenith of their reputation and political influence. A great deal has changed since then. The Schmoller *Festschrift* had the sound of a fanfare. The Brentano *Festschrift* is calling for discussion.

# 2.
# Socialism of the Chair

Academic socialism is no homogeneous ideology. In the way syndicalism stands alongside socialism, although they often are not differentiated distinctly, there are two schools of thought in Socialism of the Chair: the Socialist School

---

6. *Festgabe für Lujo Brentano: Die Wirtschaftswissenschaft nach dem Kriege* [Economics after the war], Twenty-nine Contributions to the State of German and Foreign Research after the War; vol. I, *Economic Ideologies*; vol. II, *The Situation in Research*; edited by M.J. Bonn and M. Palyi, Munich and Leipzig, 1925. Below, I quote from these contributions, giving in the footnotes author, volume, and page number.

(state socialism or etatism), and the Syndicalist School (at times called "social liberalism").

Socialism and syndicalism are implacable antagonists, and the two ideologies stand in irreconcilable contrast to liberalism. No specious argument can ignore the fact that direct control over the means of production can only rest either with individuals, with society as a whole, or with associations of workers in each industry. Politics can never succeed in dividing direct control over certain means of production between society (the state), labor unions, or individuals. Property as direct control over means of production is indivisible. True, there can be a social order in which some means are owned by the state or other administrative bodies, some by labor unions, and some by individuals. In this sense, there can be partial socialism, partial syndicalism, and partial capitalism. But there can never be a compromise between socialism, liberalism, and syndicalism with regard to the same means of production. This fundamental and logical implacability of the three conceivable social orders has again and again been obscured in theory and politics. But no one has ever succeeded in creating a social order that could be called a synthesis, or even reconciliation, of the conflicting principles.

Liberalism is the ideology that views private property in the means of production as the only possible, or at least best conceivable foundation of human society based on division of labor. Socialism seeks to transfer the property in the means of production to the hands of organized society, the state. Syndicalism wants to transfer control over the means of production to the association of workers in the individual branches of production.[7]

State socialism (etatism, also conservative socialism) and its related systems of military socialism and Christian socialism aim at bringing about a society in which "the management of property is left to individuals," but its employ-

---

7. Syndicalism as a social ideal must not be confused with syndicalism as tactics. The specific syndicalistic tactics (the *action directe* of the French syndicalists) may also serve other ideologies. For instance, they may be used toward the realization of socialism.

74

ment is supervised and guided by the collective whole so that "formally property is private, but in substance it is public."[8] The farmer, for instance, becomes a "civil servant and must grow what the country needs according to his best knowledge and conscience or by government order. If he receives his interest and a living salary, he has everything he can demand."[9] Some large enterprises are transferred directly to the state or community, all others formally remain in the hands of their owners, but must be managed in accordance with the plan of the authorities. Thus, every business becomes a public office, and every occupation an "appointment."

At the time serious consideration was still given to the Social-Democratic program to transfer formally all means of production to society, there seemed to exist a considerable, although not fundamental, difference between the program of the etatists and that of the Social Democrats. Today the Social-Democratic program simply calls for an immediate nationalization of large enterprises, while trade shops and farms are to be under the control of the state. In this respect, etatists and socialists are much closer today than they were a dozen years ago.

However, the fundamental difference between the social ideals of etatism and the Social Democrats existed in the problem of income distribution, not in the nationalization program. It was self-evident to the Social Democrats that all income differences were to disappear. But etatism meant to distribute income according to "dignity." Everyone was to receive according to his rank. On this point as well, the gap dividing Social Democrats and etatists has narrowed considerably.

Etatism, too, is genuine socialism, although it may differ

---

8. Also in the restructuring of society by Othmar Spann, *Der wahre Staat* [The true state], Leipzig, 1921, p. 249. Cf. Honigheim, *Romantische und religiös-mystisch verankerte Wirtschaftsgesinnungen* [Romantic and religiously-mystically rooted economic opinions], vol. I, p. 264.
9. See Philipp von Arnim, *Ideen zu einer vollständigen Landwirtschaftlichen Buchhaltung* [Ideas on complete agricultural accounting], 1805, quoted by Waltz, *Vom Reinertrag in der Landwirtschaft* [On the net return in agriculture], Stuttgart and Berlin, 1904, p. 21.

in a few points from the socialism of the *Communist Manifesto* and the Erfurt Program. What is essential alone is its position on the problem of private property in the means of production. Inasmuch as the Socialists of the Chair represented etatism, and inasmuch as they demanded the nationalization of large enterprises and government supervision and control of all other enterprises, they engaged in socialistic politics.

But not all Socialists of the Chair were etatists. Lujo Brentano and his School promoted a syndicalistic program, although in many questions of daily politics they joined ranks with the other Socialists of the Chair and, together with the Social Democrats, fought against liberalism. As set forth, their syndicalism is no more definite and straightforward than any other program. As a matter of fact, it is so contradictory and leads to such absurd consequences that it could never be unswervingly advocated. Brentano carefully veiled his position, but nevertheless it was syndicalism. It became visible in his position on the problems of labor union coercion and strike, and the protection of workers willing to work.

If employees receive the right to shut down an enterprise as long as its owner rejects their demands, the control over production, in final analysis, has been placed in the hands of labor unions. The problem must not be obscured by the confusion between free collective bargaining—the workers' freedom to organize—and the impunity of workers guilty of breach of contract. The protection of workers willing to work is an entirely different matter. As long as the work stoppage of the workers of one enterprise or in an entire industry can be rendered ineffective through employment of workers from other industries or from a given reservoir of unemployed workers, the labor unions are unable to raise wage rates above those paid without them. But as soon as the physical force of labor, with tacit consent or open promotion by the state, makes it impossible to replace the strikers, the labor unions can do as they like. The workers of "essential" enterprises then can freely determine their wage rates. They could raise them as high as they please were it not necessary to be mindful of public opinion and the senti-

76

ment of workers in other industries. At any rate, all labor unions have the power temporarily to raise wage rates above those the economic situation would determine without union intervention.

Anyone who would deny protection to workers willing to work must raise the question of how excessive labor demands can be dealt with. It is no answer to refer to a sensible conduct of workers or to entrust committees of employers and employees with the power of decision. Committees with equal representation of both sides can come to an agreement only if one side makes the concessions. But if the decision is to be made by the state, either as judge with the power of binding arbitration or by the committee member representing the state, the solution again is that of etatism, the very thing that was to be avoided.

A social order that refuses to protect those willing to work lacks vitality and must disintegrate in short order. This is why all political systems, no matter how they collaborate with the unions, must finally oppose union coercion. To be sure, prewar Germany never managed to legislate government protection to those willing to work; an attempt failed on account of the resistance by Brentano and his School. But it should be noted that prewar Germany could easily have quashed a strike in essential enterprises by calling the strikers to active military duty. Postwar republican Germany no longer has this power at its disposal. And yet, despite the Social-Democratic Party's supremacy, it has successfully taken a stand against strikes in essential enterprises and thus has expressly granted protection to workers willing to work. In the Russia of the Soviets, a strike is utterly impossible. Kautsky and Lenin completely agree that willing workers must be permitted to render a strike against vital facilities ineffective.

Etatism trusts in the wisdom and attitude of government officials. "Our officials are learning soon enough," writes Knapp,

> how things look in the clash of economic interests. They will not let the reins slip out of their hands, not even to parliamentary majorities, which we

know how to handle so well. No rule is born so easily, in fact, perceived so gratefully as that of high-minded, very learned officials. The German state is officialdom, let us hope that it will always remain that. It should then be rather easy to overcome the confusion and error of economic struggles.[10]

Brentano and his School lacked this faith in the infallibility of government officials, on which they based their very claim to being "liberal." But over the years, the two schools have come very close: the Brentano School advocated nationalization or municipalization of a number of enterprises, and the Schmoller School emphasized the activity of labor unions. For a long time, their positions on foreign trade policies separated the two schools. Brentano rejected protectionism, while the majority of etatists pursued it. On this point the etatists have made some concessions; an ambiguous free-trade resolution, devised in 1923 by university professors meeting at Stuttgart, revealed this change.

Brentano himself sought to describe their differences in the fundamental questions of social policy as follows:

> We both favored the activity of free organizations as well as government intervention wherever the individual left to his own was too weak to preserve his personality and to develop his ability. But from the beginning our positions on both were reversed. My studies of British conditions had led me to build my hopes for lifting the working classes primarily on the activities of their organizations, while it mattered much more to Schmoller that the state assume the role of protector of the weak.[11]

---

10. Knapp, *Die Landarbeiter in Knechtschaft und Freiheit* [Agricultural workers in serfdom and freedom], 2nd ed., Leipzig, 1909, p. 86; now also in *Einführung in einige Hauptfragen der Nationalökonomie* [Introduction to a few principal questions of economics], Munich and Leipzig, 1925, p. 1922.

11. Brentano, *Ist das System Brentano zusaummengebrochen?* [Has the Brentano system collapsed?], Berlin, 1918, p. 14 *et seq.*

Brentano wrote this in the spring of 1918, shortly after the collapse of the Schmoller system, and·shortly before the collapse of the Brentano system became evident. While the fundamental differences between the two schools are not clearly delineated, they are at least discernible.

# 3.
# Liberalism and Social Liberalism

Names are unimportant; what matters is substance. The term "social liberalism" sounds strange indeed as socialism and liberalism are mutually exclusive. But we are accustomed to such terminology. Also, socialism and democracy are irreconcilable in the final analysis, and yet there is the old concept of "Social Democracy," which is a *contradictio in adjecto*. If today the Brentano School, which adopted syndicalism, and some "moderate" etatists designate their movement as "social liberalism," no terminological objection need be raised. But we must object—not for political reasons, but in the interest of scientific clarity and logical thought—that this designation erases the differences between liberalism and socialism. It permits calling "liberal" that which is the very opposite of what history and social science define as liberal. The fact that in Great Britain, the home of liberalism, this semantic confusion prevails is no excuse for us to accede to the practice.

Herkner is correct when he observes that the sanctity of private property is not a dogmatically anchored objective for liberalism, but a means for the attainment of ultimate goals. He is mistaken, however, when he states that this is so

79

"only temporarily."[12] In their highest and ultimate goal liberalism and socialism are in agreement. They differ precisely in that liberalism views private property in the means of production as the most suitable means to attain the goal, while socialism looks upon public property as the most suitable means. This difference in the two programs, and this alone, corresponds to the history of thought during the nineteenth century. Their different positions on the problem of property in production separates liberalism from socialism. It is confusing to present this in any other way.

Socialism, according to Herkner, "is an economic system in which society organized in a state directly assumes responsibility for the existence of all its members. As an economic system based on satisfying the national needs rather than gleaning profits, the whole production and distribution process becomes the task of public authority, replacing private property in the means of production and their use for profit."[13] This is not very precise, but is stated clearly enough. Herkner then continues, "If this system could be realized with liberal means, that is, without force and violation of law, and if it could not only improve the material conditions of the people, but also assure a greater measure of individual freedom, then no objection could be raised against it from the liberal point of view."[14] Thus, when Parliament discusses the question of nationalization, the liberals, according to Herkner, could vote for the common weal if it is introduced "without force and violation of law" and if it were not for their doubts about the material well-being of the people.

Herkner seems to believe that the older liberalism advocated private property for its own sake and not for its social consequences. Like Wiese and Zwiedineck, he construes a difference between the older and the contemporary liberalism. According to Herkner, "While the older liberalism viewed private property as an institution of natural law

12. Herkner, "Socialpolitischer Liberalismus" [Social liberalism], vol. I, p. 41.
13. *Ibid.*, vol. I, p. 43.
14. *Ibid.*, p. 44.

whose protection besides that of individual freedom was the first duty of the state, contemporary liberalism is emphasizing ever more strongly the social factor in property. . . . Private property is no longer defended with individualistic reasons, but with considerations of social and economic suitability."[15] In a similar vein, Zwiedineck observes that there is reason for optimism "that a private property order for its own sake and in the interest of owners only, would be of brief duration." Modern liberalism, too, is advocating private property on grounds of "social suitability."[16]

It cannot be our task here to examine how nonliberal theories of natural law meant to defend private property as a natural phenomenon. But it should be common knowledge that the older liberals were utilitarians (they are frequently criticized for it), and that it was self-evident to them that no social institution and no ethical rule can be advocated for its own sake or for reasons of special interest, but can be defended only on grounds of social suitability. It is no indication that liberalism is moving toward socialism if modern liberalism demands private property in the means of production because of its social utility, and not for its own sake or for the interests of owners.

"Private property and inheritance," Herkner continues, "give rise to unearned income. Liberalism sympathizes with the efforts of socialists to oppose this unearned income in the interest of justice and equal opportunity for all members of society."[17] The fact that unearned income flows from property is as obvious as that poverty comes from *pauvreté*. In fact, unearned income flows from control over the means of production. He who opposes unearned income must oppose private property in the means of production. Therefore, a liberal cannot sympathize with such efforts. If he does so nevertheless, he is no longer a liberal.

---

15. *Ibid.*, p. 49.
16. Zwiedineck-Südenhorst, "Zur Eigentums- und Produktionsverfassung" [On the organization of property and production], vol. II, p. 447.
17. Herkner, vol. I, p. 49.

What in Herkner's view, then, is liberalism? His answer is this:

> Liberalism is a world view, a kind of religion, a faith. It is a faith in the natural dignity and goodness of man, in his great destiny, in his ability to grow through his powers of natural reason and freedom, in the victory of justice and truth. Without freedom there is no truth. Without truth there can be no triumph of justice, no progress, thus no development, later stages of which are always more desirable than the preceding stages. What sunlight and oxygen mean to organic life, reason and freedom mean to intellectual development. Neither individuals, classes, nations, nor races must be viewed as mere means for the purposes of other individuals, classes, nations or races. [18]

This is all very fine and noble, but unfortunately so general and vague that it equally applies to socialism, syndicalism, and anarchism. His definition of liberalism lacks the decisive ingredient, namely, a social order that is built on private property in the means of production.

It cannot surprise us that with such ignorance about liberalism Herkner also subscribes to practically all misconceptions that are in vogue today. Among others: "In contrast to the older liberalism which aimed mainly at the elimination of hampering restrictions, modern liberalism [that is, social liberalism] has a positive, constructive program." [19] If Herkner had discovered private property in the means of production as the basic ingredient of liberalism, he would have known that the liberal program is no less positive and constructive than any other. It is the mentality of officialdom—which, according to Brentano, was "the only sounding-board of the Association for Social Policy" [20]— that considers as constructive and positive only that ideol-

---

18. *Ibid.*, p. 39.
19. *Ibid.*, p. 47.
20. Brentano, *op. cit.*, p. 19.

ogy which calls for the greatest number of offices and officials. And he who seeks to reduce the number of state agents is decried as a "negative thinker" or an "enemy of the state."

Both Herkner and Wiese[21] expressly emphasize that liberalism has nothing to do with capitalism. Passow tried to show that the ambiguous terms "capitalism," "capitalistic economic order," et cetera, are political slogans that, with but few exceptions, are not used objectively to classify and comprehend the facts of economic life. Instead, they are used to criticize, accuse, and condemn phenomena that are more or less misunderstood.[22] If this position is taken, it is clear that he who appreciates liberalism, no matter how he defines it, seeks to protect it from labels that are felt to be derogatory, defamatory, and abusive. However, if we agree with Passow's observation that for most writers who have given the term "capitalism" a definite meaning, its essence is the development and expansion of larger enterprises,[23] we must admit that liberalism and capitalism are closely related. It was liberalism that created the ideological conditions that gave rise to modern large-scale industrial production. If we should use the term capitalism to identify an economic method that arranges economic activity according to capital calculation,[24] we must come to the same conclusion. But no matter how we define capitalism, the development of capitalistic methods of production was and is possible only within the framework of a social order built on private property in the means of production. Therefore, we cannot agree with Wiese's contention that the essence of liberalism was obscured by "its historical coincidence with large-scale capitalism."[25]

That which makes capitalism appear "unliberal," according to Wiese, is "its insensitivity toward suffering, the bru-

---

21. See Herkner, vol. I, p. 38; Wiese, "Gibt es noch Liberalismus?" [Is there still liberalism?], vol. I, p. 22.
22. See Passow, *Kapitalismus* [Capitalism], Jena, 1918, p. 1 *et seq.*
23. *Ibid.*, p. 132 *et seq.*
24. See my *Gemeinwirtschaft*, Jena, 1922, p. 110 *et seq.* [English-language edition: *Socialism* (London: Jonathan Cape, 1936), p. 111 *et seq.*]
25. Wiese, *op. cit.*, vol. I, p. 23.

tal use of elbows, and the struggle to overpower and enslave fellow men."[26] These expressions come from the old register of socialistic complaints about the corruption and wickedness of capitalism. They reveal the socialistic misinterpretation of the nature and substance of a social order that is based on private property. If, in a capitalistic society, the buyer seeks to buy an economic good wherever it is least expensive, without regard for other considerations, he does not act with "insensitivity toward suffering." If the superior enterprise successfully competes with one working less economically, there is no "brutal use of elbows," or "struggle to overpower and enslave fellow men." The process in this case is no undesirable concomitant effect, or "outgrowth" of capitalism, and unwanted by liberalism. On the contrary! The sharper the competition, the better it serves its social function to improve economic production. That the stagecoach driver was replaced by the railroad, the hand weaver by mechanical weaving, the shoemaker by the shoe factory, did not happen contrary to the intentions of liberalism. And when small shipowners with sailing vessels were replaced by a large steamship company, when a few dozen butchers were replaced by a slaughterhouse, a few hundred merchants by a department store, it signifies no "overpowering and enslaving of fellow men."

Wiese remarks correctly that "in reality, liberalism has never existed on a large scale, and that the community of liberals still needs to be created and brought along."[27] Thus, the picture of what fully developed capitalism can achieve is incomplete at best, even if we reflect upon British society at the zenith of capitalism when liberalism was leading the way. It is popular today to blame capitalism for anything that displeases. Indeed, who is still aware of what he would have to forego if there were no "capitalism"? When great dreams do not come true, capitalism is charged immediately. This may be a proper procedure for party politics, but in scientific discussion it should be avoided.

---

26. *Ibid.*
27. *Ibid.*, p. 16.

# 4.
# Control or
# Economic Law?

Among the many mistakes to which the Socialists of the Chair of all varieties tenaciously cling is their faith in limited government interventions in economic life. They are convinced that, except for syndicalism, there are three conceivable possibilities of control over the means of production in a society based on the division of labor. Besides public property and private property, there is the third possibility of private property that is subject to government regulation. The possibility and conceivability of this third system will be discussed in this section on the antithesis of "control or economic law."

For the Socialists of the Chair this question had special political significance. They could maintain their claim of an impartial middle position between the Manchester School and communism only if they favored a social ideal that apparently was "equally distant" from the ideals of the two competing movements. They rejected as irrelevant for their ideals all criticism leveled at the socialistic ideal. They could do so as long as they ignored the fact that limited interventions in the private property order fail to achieve their objectives, and that the desired etatist objectives can be achieved only when private property exists in name only and a central authority regulates all production. Moeller observes correctly that the younger Historical School opposed classical economics for practical reasons: "Schmoller did not care to see his road to scientific justification of social policy blocked by the concept of an external economic regularity independent of man." But Moeller is mistaken when he comments on Rist's remark that the classical school did not uphold the general validity of economic laws. He is mistaken when he asserts that "it was not the 'laws' of classical economics properly understood that were blocking the way."[28] Indeed, they stood in the way because they revealed that government intervention in the operations of a capitalistic social order is incapable of achieving the desired results, which leaves the alternative either to renounce such intervention or go the whole way and assume control over the means of production. On this fact all the critique by the Historical-Realistic School missed its mark. It was irrelevant that these economic laws were not "natural laws" and that private property was not eternal, but "only" a historical-legal category. The new economics should have replaced the theory of catallactics developed by Physiocrats and classical economists with another system that did not demonstrate the futility of government intervention. Because it could not do so, it had to reject categorically all "theoretical" investigations of economic problems.

At times it has been said that there are several kinds of economics. This is no more correct than that there are several biologies and several physics. Surely in every science various hypotheses, interpretations, and arguments seek to solve concrete problems. But logic is consistent in every science. It is true also of economics. The Historical-Realistic School itself, which for political reasons disagreed with the traditional and modern theories, proves this point by not substituting its own explanations for the rejected doctrines, but by merely denying the possibility of theoretical knowledge.

Economic knowledge necessarily leads to liberalism. On the one hand, it demonstrates that there are only two possibilities for the property problem of a society based on the division of labor: private property or public property in the means of production. The so-called middle of the road of "regulated" property is either illogical, because it does not lead to the intended goal and accomplishes nothing but a disruption of the capitalistic production process, or it must lead to complete socialization of the means of production.

---

28. Moeller, "Zur Frage der 'Objectivität' des wirtschaftlichen Prinzips" [On the "objectivity" of economic principles], *Archives for Social Science*, vol. 47, p. 163.

On the other hand, it demonstrates what has been perceived clearly only recently, that a society based on public property is not viable because it does not permit monetary calculation and thus rational economic action. Therefore, economic knowledge is blocking the way to socialistic and syndicalistic ideologies that prevail all over the world. And this explains the war that is waged everywhere against economics and economists.

Zwiedineck-Südenhorst seeks to give the untenable doctrine of the third possible social order a new garb. "We are dealing not only with the institution of property," he informs us,

> but probably more importantly also with the totality of legal standards that form a superstructure over any property order and thereby any economic order. We must realize that these legal standards are decisive for the manner of cooperation of the various factors of production (that is, not only capital, land, and labor, but also the different categories of human labor). In short, we are dealing with that which comprises the organization of production. This organization can only serve the objective of placing the momentary control conditions over the various production factors in the service of the whole economy. Only then does it have social character. Of course, these momentary control conditions, that is, the property order, constitute a part of the organization of production. But this does not lead to the conclusion that the organization would have to differ for the individualistic and the collectivistic economy. In fact, whether and how it can differ is the crucial question.[29]

Here again, as with all representatives of etatism, is the notion that a legal structure placing private property "in the service of the whole economy" can achieve the objectives

---

29. Zwiedineck-Südenhorst, *op. cit.*, vol. II, p. 430 *et seq.*

the authority meant to achieve. After all, Zwiedineck only recently took his position on the problem of "control or economic law," which is so characteristic of all Socialists of the Chair.[30]

It is remarkable that all these literary efforts produced nothing new. Old errors that had been refuted a hundred times were dished up again. The question is not whether the power of the state "can" intervene in economic life. No economist would deny today that, for instance, the bombing of a city or a prohibition of exports is possible. Even the freetrader does not deny that import duties are possible; he only maintains that protective tariffs do not have the effects the protectionists ascribe to them. And he who rejects price controls for being unsuitable does not deny that government can impose and supervise them. He merely denies that the controls will lead to the goal which government meant to attain.

# 5.
# The *Methodenstreit*

As early as the 1870s Walter Bagehot irrefutably exploded the arguments with which the followers of the Historical School rejected the dependability of "theoretical" inquiries in the field of economics. He called the two methods—the Historical School considered them the only permissible methods—the "all-case method" and the "single-case method." The former works with induction only, and makes the erroneous assumption that this is the road that usually leads the natural sciences to their findings. Bagehot demon-

---

30. See Zwiedineck-Südenhorst, "Macht oder ökonomisches Gesetz" [Control or economic law], Schmoller's *Yearbook*, 49th year, p. 273-92.

strated that this road is completely impassable, and that on it no science ever has achieved satisfactory results. The "single-case method," which accepts descriptions of concrete historical data only, fails to realize, according to Bagehot, that there can be no economic history and no economic description "unless there was a considerable accumulation of applicable doctrine before existing."[31]

The *Methodenstreit* has long been decided. Never before has a scientific exchange led to such a crushing defeat of one side. Fortunately, this is freely admitted in *Economics After the War*. In his contribution on business cycle research, which is based on a thorough knowledge of the material, Löwe briefly touches upon the question of method and skillfully proves the untenableness of the objections empiricists raise against theory. Unfortunately, we must also agree with Löwe where he observes that "the heresy of 'impartial' data research, which deprived a whole generation of German scholars of its results," has recently also intruded itself into American research.[32] But it is even more regrettable that despite the thorough methodological debates in recent years, we again and again encounter the old, long-refuted errors in German science. Bonn, for instance, praises Brentano because in his book on *Agricultural Policy* he was not content with "describing the skeleton of a system, separated from the flesh of life. He abhored bloodless abstractions, deductions of barren concepts, as he encountered them in his youth. He sought the fullness of life."[33]

I must admit that I find the term "flesh of life" empty. Bonn's use of the adjective "bloodless" in connection with the noun "abstraction" appears illogical to me. What is the contrast to "bloodless" abstraction—perhaps "bloody" abstraction? No science can avoid abstract concepts, and he who abhors them should stay away from science and see whether and how he can go through life without them.

31. Bagehot, "The Postulates of English Political Economy," in *Works*, edited by Russell Barrington, London, 1915, vol. VII, p. 100-104.
32. Löwe, "Der gegenwärtige Stand der Konjunkturforschung in Deutschland" [The present state of business cycle research in Germany], vol. II, p. 365 *et seq.*
33. Bonn, "Geleitwort: Lujo Brentano als Wirtschaftspolitiker" [Preface: Lujo Brentano as economic politician], vol. I, p. 4.

When we look at Brentano's *Agricultural Policy* we find a number of discussions of rent, land price, cost, et cetera, purely theoretical investigations that obviously work with abstractions and abstract concepts.[34] Every investigation that in any way touches upon economic questions must "theorize." True, the empiricist does not know that he is theorizing, as Monsieur Jourdain never knew that he was always speaking prose. And as empiricists are unaware of this, they carelessly adopt theories that are incomplete or even incorrect and avoid thinking them through logically. An explanatory theory can easily be constructed for each "fact," but only when the individual theories are united into a whole can we determine the value and futility of the "explanation." But the Historical School rejected it all; it did not want to admit that theories must be thought through and that they must be united into a consistent whole. In eclectic fashion it used pieces of all possible theories and followed indiscriminately and uncritically now this opinion, now that opinion.

But the Socialists of the Chair not only did not build a system of their own, they also failed utterly in their critique of modern theoretical economics. The subjective-value theory did not receive the outside critique that is so indispensible for scientific progress. It owes its progress during the last decades to its own initiative, to critiques from its own ranks. This the followers of the Historical School did not even notice. Whenever they speak of modern economics their eyes are glued on 1890, when the achievements of Menger and Böhm-Bawerk were generally completed. The theoretical accomplishments in Europe and America since then remain rather foreign to them.

The critique which the champions of academic socialism leveled at theoretical economics proved to be largely irrelevant and, without apparent reason, not free of personal hatred. As in the writings of Marx and his disciples, a more or less tasteful joke often takes the place of critique. Brentano thought it proper to introduce a critique of Böhm-Ba-

34. See Brentano, *Agrarpolitik* [Agricultural policy], Stuttgart, 1897, pp. 60 *et seq.*, 83 *et seq.*

werk's *Capital and Interest*—a critique which, by the way, no one appreciated in the seventeen years since its publication —with the following: "As one of my first-semester students correctly remarked. . . ."[35] The Russian professor Totomianz, an Armenian, writes in his *History of Economics and Socialism:*

> A German critic of the psychological school ironically observes, not without a kernel of truth, that the soil in which the Austrian School grew was the city of Vienna with its numerous students and officers. For a young student seeking the pleasures of life present goods naturally are more valuable than future goods. Similarly, a dashing officer chronically suffering from lack of cash will pay any interest rate on borrowed money.[36]

This book with such a profound critique of Böhm-Bawerk's theory first appeared in the Russian language. Rist wrote an introduction to the French edition, Loria to the Italian edition, and Masaryk to the Czech edition. In his introduction to the German edition, Herkner acclaims the work for being "popular and perceptual." All significant and fruitful thoughts in Great Britain, France, Germany, Austria, Belgium, Italy, Russia, and America find "loving and under-

---

35. Brentano, *Konkrete Grundbedingungen der Volkswirtschaft* [Concrete conditions of economy], Leipzig, 1924, p. 113.

36. V. Totomianz, *Geschichte der Nationalökonomie und des Socialismus* [History of economics and socialism], Jena, 1925, p. 152. Even if we disregard this critique of Böhm-Bawerk, the Totomianz effort is wholly unsatisfactory and mistaken. He states, for instance, on p. 146: "While Menger's achievement mainly was the development of a new methodology, the two other representatives of the Austrian School, Böhm-Bawerk and Wieser, built a sagacious psychological value theory." We must conclude from this statement that Menger contributed less to the development of the new value theory than Böhm-Bawerk and Wieser, which is not at all correct. Totomianz introduces his discussion of the marginal utility theory with the following statement: "The economy consists of economic goods. These goods relate in a certain way to human well-being. This relationship is expressed in two different grades or stages: the lower stage and the higher stage. We are dealing with the higher stage when the economic good is not only useful, but also necessary for well-being, so that its possession or loss entails a loss of consumption or enjoyment." His discussion of other economists is not better. As I do not read Russian, I cannot determine whether this nonsense must be charged to the Russian original or to the German translation.

standing consideration" with Totomianz. He shows "remarkable ability to do justice to such different minds as Fourier, Ruskin, Marx, Rodbertus, Schmoller, Menger, and Gide."[37] This Herkner judgment is all the stranger as he is very familiar with the history of economic thought.[38]

In the *Methodenstreit* the Brentano wing of the Empirical-Realistic School acted more prudently than the followers of Schmoller. We must give personal credit to Brentano who, a generation earlier, leveled sharp criticism at the School's research in economic history.

> Many a writer of no more than excerpts from economic documents believes he has written an economic treatise. But when the excerpt is completed the economic analysis is just beginning. Its content must then be analyzed and transformed to a picture full of life, and the lesson must be drawn from this researched passage of life. It is not enough to be diligent in the preparation of excerpts from documents. It takes the power of intuition, combination, sagacity, and *the most important scientific gift: the ability to recognize the common element in the multiplicity of phenomena.* When this is lacking we gain nothing but uninteresting details. . . . This kind of economic historical analysis is utterly worthless for economics.[39]

And bearing in mind the etatist bias in the works of the Schmoller School, Brentano calls it an aberration "to confuse enthusiastic excerpts from archives with economic investigations and research."[40]

---

37. *Ibid.*, p. 7 *et seq.*
38. See Herkner, *Die Geschichte der Nationalökonomie, Festschrift für Lujo Brentano zum siebzigsten Geburtstag* [History of economics, *Festschrift* for Lujo Brentano in honor of his seventieth birthday], Munich and Leipzig, 1916, p. 223-35.
39. Emphasis added. Brentano, "Über den grundherrlichen Charakter des hausindustriellen Leinengewerbes in Schlesien" [On the manorial character of the linen home industry in Silesia], *Journal for Social and Economic History*, vol. I, 1893, p. 319 *et seq.*
40. *Ibid.*, p. 322.

# 6.
# The Economic Doctrines of Social Liberalism

Faithful to their principle, the Socialists of the Chair did not create a system of economics, which was the endeavor of the Physiocrats and classical economists, and now the modern subjectivist economists. The socialists were not concerned with creating a system of catallactics.

Marx simply adopted the system of the classics and drew the conclusion that, in a society based on the division of labor, there is no third organizational possibility besides the private property and the public property orders. He mocked all attempts at a third order as "bourgeois." The position of etatism is different. From the start it did not seek to understand, but to judge. It brought along preconceived ethical opinions: "It shall be!" and "It shall not be!" All things were chaotic as long as the state did not intervene. Only government intervention could put an end to the arbitrariness of self-seeking individuals. The idea that a social order could be based on a constitution under which the state would do nothing but protect private property in the means of production seemed utterly absurd to it. It only had ridicule for the "enemies of the state" who believed in such a "pre-established harmony." The etatists thought it utterly illogical to reject every government "intervention" in economic life, as this would lead to anarchism. If government intervention for the protection of private property is permissible, it is illogical to reject all further intervention. The only reasonable economic order is a social order in which private property exists in name, but actually is abolished, the state holding the final reins over production and distribution. The state of affairs at the zenith of liberalism could come into existence only because the state neglected its duties and granted too much freedom to individuals. With such a point of view, the development of a catallactic system is unnecessary, indeed illogical.

The best example for the ideology of the welfare state is the balance of payments theory. A country may lose all its monetary metal if the state does not intervene, so runs the older, mercantilist version. The classical economists demonstrated, however, that the danger so dreaded by the mercantilists does not exist, because forces are at work that, in the long run, prevent the loss of money. This is why the quantity theory was always so objectionable to etatists. They favored the Banking School. The victory of the Historical School practically brought excommunication of the Currency School. Karl Marx,[41] Adolf Wagner, Helfferich, Hilferding, Havenstein, and Bendixen held to the doctrines of the Banking School.

After two generations of eclecticism and avoidance of clear concepts, many contemporary writers have difficulty recognizing the differences between those two famous British schools. Thus Palyi shows surprise that "a resolute follower of the Banking Principle, M. Ausiaux, occasionally . . . advocates the comptabilism of Solvay."[42] Let us not overlook the fact that "comptabilism" and all other related systems are logical applications of the Banking Principle. If the banks are in no position to issue more notes than are

---

41. Marx did not recognize that by adopting the Banking Principle he acknowledged the foundation on which Proudhon's exchange-bank ideas were based. Marx had no clear conception of banking; in many cases he uncritically followed the Banking Theorists. How little he understood of the problems is visible in each of the few remarks he added to the excerpts, as, for instance, on the Catholic character of the monetary system and the Protestant character of the credit system (*Das Kapital*, vol. III, pt. II, 3rd ed., Hamburg, 1911, p. 132). Even more characteristic is another remark that connects with the basic principle of the Banking Principle that "the emission of a certain quantity of one-pound notes replaces an equal quantity of sovereigns." According to Marx, "a sleight of hand well known to all banks!" (*Ibid.*, vol. I, 7th ed., Hamburg, 1914, p. 84.) What is the purpose of this "sleight of hand"? Banks were not interested in attracting sovereigns through the issue of notes. They were interested only in granting more credits through the issue of more notes and thereby raising their interest income. This "sleight of hand" was well known to banks, but not that mentioned by Marx.
42. Palyi, "Ungelöste Fragen der Geldtheorie" [Unsolved questions of monetary theory], vol. II, p. 514.

necessary (the "elasticity of circulation"), there can be no objection to the adoption of Solvay's monetary reform.

Palyi's etatist position explains why he could not add a single word to the old mercantilist observations, and why his whole theory is limited to pointing at the selfish disposition of the state's subjects, who should not be left to themselves.[43] Social liberalism could not share this etatist position. For better or worse it had to show how, according to its social ideal, the members of an exchange society cooperate without government assistance. But social liberalism never developed a comprehensive theory either. Some of its followers probably believed that the time was not yet ripe on account of insufficient preparation through collection of material; the majority probably never saw the need for a comprehensive theory at all. Wherever the need for theory arose, the social liberals usually borrowed from the classical system, mostly in the garb of Marxism. In this regard the social liberals differed from the etatists, who preferred to fall back on the mercantilists.

Nevertheless, social liberalism did seek to make an independent contribution to theory—a doctrine of wage rates. It could use neither classical theory nor modern theory. Marx very logically had denied that collective bargaining of labor unions could raise wages. Only Brentano and Webb sought to prove that collective bargaining can permanently raise the income of all workers; this theory is the principal doctrine of social liberalism. However, it could not withstand a scientific critique, such as that by Pohle[44] and Adolf Weber.[45] In his last essay, Böhm-Bawerk, too, arrived at the same conclusion,[46] and no one today dares seriously represent the Brentano-Webb doctrine. It is significant that the

---

43. Only subjects have selfish "special interests" and do not know what is good for them. Government officials and "the sovereign" are always unselfish and wise.
44. See Pohle, *Die gegenwärtige Krisis in der deutschen Volkswirtschaftslehre* [The contemporary crisis in German economics], 2nd ed., Leipzig, 1921, p. 29 *et sea.*
45. See Adolf Weber, *Der Kampf zwischen Kapital und Arbeit* [The struggle between capital and labor], 2nd ed., Tubingen, 1920, p. 411 *et seq.*
46. Böhm-Bawerk, "Macht oder ökonomisches Gesetz" [Control or economic law], *Collected Works*, edited by Weiss, Vienna, 1924, p. 230 *et seq.* [English-language edition: *Shorter Classics of Böhm-Bawerk* (South Holland, Ill.: Libertarian Press, 1962), vol. I, p. 139 *et seq.*]

comprehensive *Festschrift* honoring Brentano does not contain a single contribution on wage theory and the wage policies of labor unions. Cassau merely observes that before the war the labor union movement worked "without any wage theory."[47]

In his review of the first edition of Adolf Weber's book, Schmoller responded to the point that it is regularly impossible, without a rise in productivity, to raise wage rates through the withholding of labor. According to Schmoller, "such theoretical abstract price discussions" could lead to no useful results. We can render a "safe judgment" only "if we can numerically measure these fine complicated processes." Adolf Weber sees in such an answer a declaration of bankruptcy of our science.[48] But the etatist need not be concerned with the bankruptcy of catallactics. In fact, the consistent etatist denies the existence of any regularity in the process of market phenomena. At any rate, as politician the etatist knows an escape from the dilemma: the state determines the level of wages. But the refutation of the Brentano-Webb doctrine alone is not fatal. Even if we were to accept it—which, as we pointed out, no one would dare do since the writings of Adolf Weber, Pohle, and Böhm-Bawerk —the decisive question would still need an answer. If labor unions actually had the power to raise the average wage of all workers above the rate that would prevail without their intervention, the question remains, How high can wages go? Can average wages go so high that they absorb all "unearned" income and must be paid out of capital? Or is there a lower limit at which this rise must stop? This is the problem the "power theory" must answer with regard to every price. But until today no one has ever tried to solve the problem.

We must not deal with the power problem by calling authoritative intervention "impossible," as did older liberal-

---

47. Cassau, *Die sozialistische Ideenwelt vor und nach dem Kriege* [The socialistic world of ideas before and after the war], vol. I, p. 136.
48. See Weber, *op. cit.*, p. 405.

ism. There cannot be any doubt that labor unions are in the position to raise wage rates as high as they wish if the state assists them by denying protection to all workers willing to work, and either pays unemployment compensation or forces employers to hire workers. But then the following occurs:

The workers in essential enterprises are in the position to extract any arbitrary wage from the rest of the population. But ignoring even that, the shifting of the wage boost to consumer prices can be borne by the workers themselves, but not by capitalists and entrepreneurs whose incomes did not rise on account of the wage boost. They now must curtail capital accumulation, or consume less, or even eat into their capital. What they will do, and to what extent they will do it, depends on the size of their income reduction. Surely everyone will agree that it is inconceivable thus to eliminate or merely greatly to curtail property income without at least reducing or halting capital formation and very likely consuming capital (after all, there is nothing in the way of unions that could keep them from raising their demands to levels that absorb all "unearned" income). But it is obvious that the consumption of capital does not permanently raise the workers' wages.

The etatist and social-liberal roads to higher wages of workers diverge. But neither leads to the goal. As social liberalism cannot possibly wish to halt or reduce capital formation, much less cause capital consumption, it finally faces the alternative: either capitalism or socialism. *Tertium non datur* ("There is no third road").

# 7.
# The Concept
# and Crisis of
# Social Policy

All the economic policies of the last two generations are designed step by step to abolish private property in the means of production— if not in name, then in substance— and to replace the capitalist social order with a socialistic order. Decades ago Sidney Webb announced it in his *Fabian Essays*.[49] As the pictures of the desired future social order varied with the individual branches of socialism, so did their opinions on the road by which the goal was to be reached. There are questions on which all branches could agree. In other questions great differences separated the camps, as, for instance, factory labor by married women, or protection of handcrafts from the competition of big business. But they all agreed on the rejection of the social ideal of liberalism. No matter how they differed from each other, they joined ranks in the fight against "Manchesterism." In this point, at least, the champion Socialists of the Chair saw eye to eye with the champions of social liberalism.

For the movement toward a gradual replacement of capitalism by a socialistic or syndicalistic social order, the term "social policy" slowly gained acceptance. A precise definition of the term was never offered, as sharp conceptual definitions were never the concern of the Historical School. The use of the term "social policy" remained ambiguous. Only in recent years when pressed by economic critique did the social politicians attempt to define the term.

---

49. Sidney Webb, *Die historische Entwicklung* [Historical development], edited by Grunwald, Leipzig, 1897, p. 44.

Sombart probably recognized the nature of social policy most clearly. "By social policy," he wrote in 1897, "we understand those measures of economic policy that effect the preservation, promotion, or repression of certain economic systems."[50] Amonn rightly found many faults with this definition, but especially pointed out that measures should be characterized by their objectives, not by their effects within the framework of policy, and that social policy goes beyond the realm that usually is called "economic policy."[51] But it is decisive that Sombart saw a change in the economic order as the objective of social policy. Let us bear in mind that when he wrote this, Sombart was standing firmly on Marxian ground, which made him think of the introduction of socialism as the only conceivable social policy. We must admit that he correctly perceived the essential point. The only deficiency of his definition is his inclusion of all efforts toward a realization of the liberal program, efforts that were made at a time when, in the language of Marx, the bourgeoisie was still a revolutionary class. Similarly, Sombart expressly included the liberation of peasants from feudal servitude as an example of social policy. Many writers followed him in this respect. Again and again they sought to define the term "social policy" in such a way that it would include political measures other than those aiming at the realization of socialism.[52]

It makes little sense to deal further with the empty argument on the concept of social policy, an argument that just recently caught fire. It was touched off by the crisis that seized socialism and syndicalism of all varieties upon the victory of the Marxian Social Democrats in Germany.

Prussian etatism and its intellectual followers in other countries, had gone as far on the road to socialism as possi-

50. Sombart, "Ideale der Sozialpolitik" [Ideals of social policy], *Archives for Social Legislation and Statistics,* vol. X, p. 8 *et seq.*
51. See Amonn, "Der Begriff der Sozialpolitik" [The concept of social policy], Schmoller's *Yearbook,* 48th year, 1924, p. 160 *et seq.*
52. It is characteristic that the Historical School, which otherwise knows only of historical categories, seeks to define the concept of social policy so that they may speak also of old Babylonian and Aztecan social policy.

ble without too much visible damage to the economy and too great a reduction in the productivity of labor. No one whose vision is unclouded by party politics can deny that Prussia-Germany of the prewar era was more suited than any other country before or since to conduct socialistic experiments. The tradition of Prussian officialdom, the faith of all educated people in the calling of the state, the military-hierarchic classification of the population, its inclination to blindly obey the authorities, all provided the prerequisites for socialism given nowhere else. Never can there be men more suited for the management of a socialistic communal operation than the mayors of German cities or the directors of the Prussian railroad. They did everything possible to make communal enterprises work. If, in spite of these advantages the system failed, it proved conclusively that the system just cannot be realized.

Suddenly the Social Democrats came to power in Germany and Austria. For many decades they had announced time and again that their genuine socialism had nothing in common with the false socialism of the etatists, and that they would proceed completely differently from the bureaucrats and professors. Now was the time to demonstrate what they could do. But they could not come up with anything new except the term "socialization." In 1918 and 1919, all political parties in Germany and Austria added the socialization of suitable industries to their programs. At that time no step on the way to pure socialism of the Marxian variety met serious resistance. Even so, what was realized did not exceed in direction or scope that which the Socialists of the Chair had recommended earlier, or in many cases had already tried. Only a few day-dreamers in Munich believed that the example of Lenin and Trotsky in agrarian Russia could be emulated in industrial Germany without causing an unprecedented crisis.

Socialism did not fail because of ideological resistance— the prevailing ideology is socialistic even today. It failed because of its unrealizability. As the general awareness grew that every step taking us away from the private property order always reduced labor's productivity, and so brought want and misery, it became necessary not only to halt the advance to socialism, but even to repeal some of the socialistic measures already taken. Even the Soviets had to yield. They did not proceed with the socialization of land, but merely distributed the land to the rural population. In trade and commerce they replaced pure socialism with the "New Economic Policy." However, the ideology did not participate in this retreat. It stubbornly clung to its pronouncements of decades ago, and sought to explain the failures of socialism in all possible ways except the right one—its basic unrealizability.

Only a few champions of socialism have realized that the failure of socialism was not coincidental, but inevitable. Some went even further and admitted that all social measures reduce productivity, consume capital and wealth, and are destructive. The renunciation of the ideals these men used to embrace is called in economic literature the crisis of social policy.[53] In reality, it is much more: it is the great world crisis of destructionism—the policy that seeks to destroy the social order based on private property in the means of production.

The world can support teeming humanity in the manner in which it has been supported in recent decades only if men work capitalistically. Only capitalism can be expected to further raise the productivity of human labor. The fact that the vast majority of people adheres to an ideology that refuses to admit this, and therefore conducts policies that lead to a reduction of labor productivity and consumption of capital, is the essence of the great cultural crisis.

---

53. See Pribram, "Die Wandlungen des Begriffes der Sozialpolitik" [The changes in the concept of social policy], vol. II, p. 249.

# 8.
# Max Weber
# and the Socialists
# of the Chair

The opposition that arose in Germany against the Socialists of the Chair generally started with an awareness that
theoretical investigations of economic problems are essential. As economists, Dietzel, Julius Wolf, Ehrenberg, Pohle,
Adolf Weber, Passow, and others rose against the Socialists
of the Chair. On the other hand, historians raised objections
against the manner in which Schmoller, Knapp, and his pupils sought to solve historical tasks. Equipped with the tools
of their sciences, these critics approached the doctrines of
the Socialists of the Chair from the outside. Of course the
Socialists of the Chair, with their great prestige and important positions, made it difficult for the critics; but the encounter presented no problem of conscience to them. They
either had never been under the spell of socialism, or had
freed themselves from it without difficulty.

It was quite different with Max Weber. To the younger
Max Weber, the ideas of Prussian etatism, the Socialism of
the Chair, and evangelical social reform had meant everything. He had absorbed them before he had begun to deal
scientifically with the problems of socialism. Religious,
political, and ethical considerations had determined his
position.

Max Weber's university training was in law; his early
scientific works dealt with legal history. He began as an un-
salaried lecturer and became professor of law. His inclination was for history, not the historical research of particulars
that is lost in details and overlooks the whole, but universal
history, historical synthesis, and the philosophy of history.

To him, history was no goal in itself, but a means toward gaining more profound political insights. Economics was alien to him. He was appointed professor of economics without having dealt with this science before, which was a customary procedure at that time.[54] It reflected the Empirical-Realistic School's opinion on the nature of "social sciences" and on the scientific expertise of legal historians. Just before his untimely death Weber regretted that his knowledge of modern theoretical economics and the classical system was too limited. He mentioned his fear that time would not permit him to fill these regrettable gaps.

When he accepted the position, he was obliged to give lectures on those problems which the Socialists of the Chair considered the proper subject matter for university teaching. But Weber found no satisfaction in the prevailing doctrine. The jurist and historian in him rebelled against the manner in which the School treated legal and historical problems. This is why he began his pioneering methodological and epistemological investigations. It led him to the problems of materialistic philosophy of history, from which he then approached the religious-sociological tasks. He proceeded finally to a grandiose attempt at a system of social sciences.

But all these studies, step by step, led Max Weber away from the political and social ideals of his youth. He moved, for the first time, toward liberalism, rationalism, utilitarianism. It was a painful personal experience, not different from that of many other scholars breaking away from Christianity. Indeed, his faith and religion were Prussian etatism; breaking away from it was like desertion from hope, his own people, indeed, from European civilization.

As it became clear to him that the prevailing social ideology was untenable, and as he saw where it was bound to lead he began to see the future of the German nation and the other nations that carry European civilization. In a way, as

54. Marianne Weber recalls of her husband's time in Freiburg: "He reports in joking exaggeration that he is listening to great economic lectures, given by himself." Marianne Weber, *Max Weber, Ein Lebensbild* [Max Weber: a biography], Tübingen, 1926, p. 213.

the *cauchemar des coalitions* ("nightmare of coalitions") deprived Bismarck of his sleep, so the recognition to which his studies led him gave Weber no rest. No matter how he clung to the hope that everything would work out in the end, a dark premonition told him again and again that a catastrophe was approaching. This awareness gnawed at his health, filled him with growing uneasiness after the outbreak of the World War, urged him on to activity that for a man unwanted by any of the political parties had to remain fruitless, and finally hastened his death.

From its beginning in Heidelberg, the life of Max Weber was an uninterrupted inner struggle against the doctrines of the Socialism of the Chair. But he did not fight this struggle to the end; he died before he succeeded in completely freeing himself from the spell of these doctrines. He died lonely, without intellectual heirs who could continue the fight he had to give up in death. To be sure, his name is praised, but the true substance of his work is not recognized, and that which was most important to him has found no disciples. Only opponents have recognized the dangers to their own ideology from the thoughts of Max Weber.[55]

# 9.
# The Failure of the Prevailing Ideology

In all variations and colors the ideas of socialism and syndicalism have lost their scientific moorings. Their cham-

---

55. See Wilbrandt, "Kritisches zu Max Webers Soziologie der Wirtschaft" [On the critique of Weber's economic sociology], *Cologne Quarterly for Sociology*, 5th year, p. 171 *et seq.*; Spann, "Bemerkungen zu Max Webers Sociologie" [Remarks on Max Weber's sociology], *Zeitschrift für Volkswirtschaft und Sozialpolitik* [Journal for economics and social policy], new series, vol. III, p. 761 *et seq.*

pions have been unable to set forth another system more compatible with their teachings and thereby refute the charge of emptiness by the theoretical economists. Therefore, they had to deny fundamentally the posibility of theoretical knowledge in the field of social science and, especially, in economics. In their denial they were content with a few critical objections to the foundation of theoretical economics. But their methodological critique as well as their objections to various theories have proven to be utterly untenable. Nothing, absolutely nothing has remained of what half a century ago Schmoller, Brentano, and their friends used to proclaim as the new science. The fact that studies in economic history can be very instructive, and that they should be undertaken, had been known before, and had never been denied.

Even during the zenith of the Historical School theoretical economics did not remain idle. The birthday of modern subjectivist theory coincided with the foundation of the Association for Social Policy. Since then, economics and social policy have confronted each other. The social scientists do not even know the foundation of the theoretical system, and have taken no notice of the significant development of theoretical knowledge in recent decades. Wherever they sought to deal with it critically, they could not get beyond the old errors already fully dealt with by Menger and Böhm-Bawerk.

But all this has not weakened the socialistic and syndicalistic ideology. Today, it is swaying the minds of people more than ever before. The great political and economic events in recent years are seen almost exclusively from its viewpoint, though of course it has failed here also. What Cassau said about the ideology of proletarian socialism applies also to that of Socialism of the Chair: All experiences of the last decade "passed by the ideology without influencing it. Never did it have more opportunities for expansion, and scarcely ever has it been as sterile as during the debates on socialization."[56] The ideology is sterile, and yet it is reigning. Even in Great Britain and the United States, classi-

---

56. Cassau, *op. cit.*, vol. I, p. 152.

cal liberalism is losing ground every day. To be sure, there are characteristic differences between the teachings of German etatism and Marxism on the one hand, and the new doctrine of salvation in the United States on the other. The phraseology of the Americans is more carefully worded than that of Schmoller, Held, or Brentano. But the Americans' aspirations basically concur with the doctrines of the Socialists of the Chair. They also share the mistaken belief that they are upholding the private property order.

When, by and large, socialism and syndicalism are in a stagnate state, when we notice some retreating steps on the road to socialism are taken, when thought is given to a limitation of labor union power, the credit can be given neither to the scientific perception of economics nor the prevailing sociology. For but a few dozen individuals all over the globe are cognizant of economics, and no statesman or politician cares about it. The social ideology even of those political parties that call themselves "middle class," is totally socialistic, etatistic, syndicalistic. If, nevertheless, socialism and syndicalism are languishing, although the prevailing ideology is demanding further progress, it is solely due to the all-too-visible decline in labor productivity as a result of every restrictive measure. Swayed by the socialistic ideologies, everyone is searching for excuses for the failure, and not for the cause. Nevertheless, the net result has been greater caution in economic policy.

Politics does not dare introduce what the prevailing ideology is demanding. Taught by bitter experience, it subconsciously has lost confidence in the prevailing ideology. In this situation, no one, however, is giving thought to replacing the obviously useless ideology with a useful one. No help is expected from reason. Some are taking refuge in mysticism, others are setting their hopes on the coming of the "strong man"—the tyrant who will think for them and care for them.

# ANTI-MARXISM[1]

In postwar Germany and Austria, a movement has been steadily gaining significance in politics and the social sciences that can best be described as Anti-Marxism. Occasionally its followers also use this label.* Their point of departure, their mode of thinking and fighting, and their goals are by no means uniform. The principal tie that unites them is their declaration of hostility toward Marxism. Mind you, they are not attacking socialism, but Marxism, which they reproach for not being the right kind of socialism, for not being the one that is true and desirable. It would also be a serious mistake to assert, as do the noisy Social-Democrat and Communist party literati, that this Anti-Marxism approves of or in any way defends capitalism and private property in the means of production. No matter what train of thought it may pursue, it is no less anticapitalistic than Marxist.

Only scientific Anti-Marxism is discussed in what follows. The Anti-Marxism of practical politics will be touched upon only insofar as it is absolutely essential for an understanding of the intellectual movement.

---

1. *Weltwirtschaftliches Archiv* [Archives for world economy], vol. 21, 1925.

* *Editor's note:* In Germany they later came to call themselves National Socialists, or Nazis.

# 1.
# Marxism in German Science

Usually only those writers can be called Marxists who, as members of a Marxian party, are obliged to indicate approval in their writings of the Marxian doctrines as canonized by party conventions. Their scholarship can be no more than "scholasticism." Their writings aim at preserving the "purity" of the true doctrine, and their proofs consist of quotations from authorities—in the final analysis Marx and Engels. Again and again they conclude that "bourgeois" science has completely collapsed, and that truth can be sought only in Marxism. Every piece of writing then closes with the reassuring remark that in the future socialistic paradise all social problems will find a very satisfactory solution.

These Marxian writings are significant only inasmuch as they have promoted the careers of their authors. They have nothing whatsoever to do with science, and, as shall be shown, not even with German science that is so greatly influenced by the doctrines of Marx. Not a single thought has emerged from the voluminous writings of the epigones. Nothing remains but horrible waste and incessant repetition. The great struggles that shook the Marxian parties—on revisionism, dictatorship, et cetera—were not scientific; they were purely political discussions. The scientific methods used to conduct them were wholly barren in the eyes of every nonscholastic. Only Marx and Engels, not one of their epigones, have affected German science.

During the 1870s and 1880s State and Chair Socialism came to power in Germany. Classical economics had left the stage. The Austrians, scorned as eccentrics, were the only writers who contributed to modern economics, which, like

Western sociology,* at first remained wholly unknown. Besides, both were suspected of Manchesterism. Only historical and descriptive-statistical compositions were permissible, and a "social" conviction, i.e., Socialism of the Chair, was the most important requirement for scholarly recognition. In spite of, and perhaps because of, this affinity, the Socialists of the Chair opposed Social Democracy. They barely paid attention to Marx and Engels, who were considered too "doctrinaire."

This began to change when a new generation came along, pupils of the men who, in 1872, had founded the Association for Social Policy. This generation had never been exposed to university lectures on theoretical economics. It knew the classical economists by name only and was convinced that they had been vanquished by Schmoller. Very few had ever read or even seen the works of Ricardo or Mill. But they had to read Marx and Engels, which became all the more necessary as they had to cope with the growing Social Democracy. They were writing books in order to refute Marx. As a result of such efforts, they themselves, and their readers, fell under the influence of Marxian ideas. Because of their ignorance in all economic and sociological theory, they were utterly defenseless against the doctrines of Marx. They rejected the harshest political demands of Marx and Engels, but adopted the theories in milder form.

This Marxism of the pupils soon reacted on the teachers. In his article "Economy, Economics and Economic Method,"² Schmoller mentions that Jevons "correctly" said of Ricardo that "he put the wagon of political economy on the wrong track." With visible satisfaction Schmoller then adds that Hasbach observed that "it was the very track which the English bourgeoisie wanted to take." For a long time during the fight of the German Historical School against the narrow-mindedness of Ricardo, Schmoller contin-

---

* *Translator's note:* In this essay, the author still used the term *sociology* for what he later called *praxeology*, the general theory of human action.

2. Schmoller, "Volkswirtschaft, Volkswirtschaftslehre und -methode" [Economy, economics and economic method], *Handwörterbuch der Staatswissenschaften* [Handbook of social sciences], 3rd ed., vol. VIII, p. 426

109

ues "many followers of the old school" believed they were walking in the methodological footsteps of Adam Smith. Thus many were not aware "that their theories had become narrow class doctrines."[3] Socialism, according to Schmoller, can be denied "neither justification for existence nor some good effects." "Born as a philosophy of social misery, it represents a branch of science that suits the interests of workers, in the same way as the post–Adam Smith natural philosophy had become a theory serving the interests of capitalists."[4]

We can clearly see how strongly Marxian notions have permeated Schmoller's ideas of the historical development of economic systems. They are even stronger with Lexis, whose interest theory, according to Engels, is "merely a paraphrase of that of Marx."[5] Böhm-Bawerk, who agreed with this Engels judgment, observed (in 1900) that Dietzel's and Stolzmann's interest theories are also closely related to Lexis' opinion, and that we often encounter similar thoughts and pronouncements in contemporary economic literature as well. It seems to be "a trend of thought that is coming into fashion."[6]

In economics, this fashion did not last too long. For the generation of men who had been the pupils of the founders of the younger Historical School, Marx was the economic theorist par excellence. But when some pupils of these pupils began to turn their attention to the problems of theoretical economics, Marx's reputation as a theorist quickly vanished. Finally, the achievements of theoretical economics abroad and in Austria during the last two decades were recognized in Germany; and it was seen how small and insignificant a position Marx occupies in the history of economics.

However, the influence of Marxism on German sociology

---

3. *Ibid.*, p. 443.

4. *Ibid.*, p. 445.

5. F. Engels, *Vorrede zum III, Band des "Kapitals"* [Preface to vol. 3 of *Das Kapital*], 3rd ed., Hamburg, 1911, p. xii *et seq.*

6. Böhm-Bawerk, *Einige strittige Fragen der Kapitalstheorie* [Some disputed questions of capital and interest], Vienna, 1900, p. 111 *et seq.*; also on Brentano, cf. O. Spann, *Der wahre Staat* [The true state], Leipzig, 1923, p. 141 *et seq.*

has continued to grow. In sociology, more so than in economics, the Germans ignored the achievements of the West. As they began rather late to deal with sociological problems they knew only one ideology: the Marxian philosophy of history and the doctrine of class warfare. It became the starting point for German sociological thought and, through the problems it posed, greatly influenced even those writers who strove to reject it most vigorously. The majority did not repudiate the doctrine itself, but merely its political and practical consequences. In most cases they characterized the Marxian doctrine either as exaggerated, or going too far, or too one-sided, and therefore sought to complete it by adding new racial and nationalistic doctrines. The basic insufficiency of the Marxian set of problems and the failure of all attempts at solving them were not seen at all. They embarked upon historical research into the origin of the Marxian social philosophy, but ignored those few possibly defensible thoughts earlier elaborated much more concisely in France and England by such men as Taine and Buckle. Moreover, their main interest then focused upon a problem utterly insignificant for science—the famous doctrine of the "withering away" of the state. In this case, as with many of their other doctrines, Marx and Engels merely meant to find a slogan for agitation. On the one hand they wanted to fight anarchism, and on the other hand they sought to demonstrate that the "nationalization" of the means of production demanded by socialism had nothing in common with the nationalization and municipalization demanded by state and municipal socialism. It was understandable from the pont of view of party politics that the etatist critique of Marxism aimed especially at this point. It seemed so inviting to reveal the inner contradiction of the Marxian social doctrine, and to confront "the enemies of the state," Marx and Engels, with a believer in the state, Lassalle.[7]

The fact that German science had rejected the utilitarian social doctrine of the eighteenth century explains the success of Marxian social doctrine in Germany.

---

7. See B. H. Kelsen, *Sozialismus und Staat* [Socialism and state], 2nd ed., Leipzig, 1923.

The theological-metaphysical social doctrine explains and postulates society from a point of view that lies beyond human experience. God, or "nature," or an objective value, want society in a certain form to reach a desired destiny. Man must follow this command. It is assumed that submission to the social body imposes sacrifices on the individual, for which he will receive no compensation other than the awareness that he has acted well, and perhaps will be rewarded in another world. The theological doctrines and some metaphysical doctrines trust that providence will guide willing men on their proper paths, and force the recalcitrants through blessed men or institutions acting on behalf of the reigning God.

Individualism opposes such a social doctrine. It demands to know from both the religious and the metaphysical positions why the individual is to be sacrificed to society. The ensuing argument that touches the foundation of the theological-metaphysical social philosophy, corresponds to the distinction so popular in Germany between the collectivistic (universalistic) social doctrine and the individualistic doctrine.[8] But it is a crucial mistake to believe that this classification has made room for all conceivable social doctrines. It has especially failed to affect modern social philosophy that was built on eighteenth century utilitarianism.

The utilitarian social doctrine does not engage in metaphysics, but takes as its point of departure the established fact that all living beings affirm their will to live and grow. The higher productivity of labor performed in division of labor, when compared with isolated action, is ever more uniting individuals to association. Society is division and association of labor. In the final analysis, there is no conflict of interest between society and the individual, as everyone can pursue his interests more efficiently in society than in isolation. The sacrifices the individual makes to society are

---

8. See Dietzel, "Individualismus," in *Handwörterbuch*, 4th ed., ch. V, p. 408 *et seq.* A. Pribram, *Die Entstehung der individualistichen Sozialphilosophie* [The development of individualistic social philosophy], Leipzig, 1912, p. 1 *et seq.* For a critique of this view, see L. von Wiese, "Dietzel's 'Individualism' " in *Kölner Vierteljahrshefte für Sozialwissenschaften* [Cologne quarterly for social sciences], Munich and Leipzig, vol. II, 1922, p. 54 *et seq.*

merely temporary, surrendering a small advantage in order to attain a greater one. This is the essence of the often cited doctrine of the harmony of interests.

The etatistic and socialistic critique never understood the "preestablished harmony" of the free trade school from Smith to Bastiat. Its theological appearance is not essential for the doctrine. Utilitarian sociology seeks to explain the development of society since man's presumably hermitic existence in prehistoric times, or since his less developed cooperation in known history. It seeks to explain man's social ties throughout history, and hopefully his future progress toward association, from principles that are active in each individual. In accordance with teleological considerations, association is thought to be "good" and laudable. A faithful soul seeking an understanding of social development views the principle of association as a wise arrangement of God. It could not be different: goodness, namely, the division of labor now and in the future, emanates from human nature. It follows that the division of labor is a good means in view of its good results, even if from different points of view it should be viewed as evil, weak, or deficient. To Adam Smith, even the weakness of man was not "without its utility." And he concludes: "Every part of nature, when attentively surveyed, equally demonstrates the providential care of its Author; and we may admire the wisdom and goodness of God even in the weakness and folly of men."[9] Obviously, the theistic tone is only an appendage, which could readily be replaced by the term "nature," as Smith does in other passages of his book where he speaks of "the great Director of Nature" or just of "nature." The social doctrines of Smith and Kant do not differ in basic attitudes and views. Kant, too, tries to explain how "nature" guides man to the goal it has set for him. The only difference between Smith and Kant consists of the fact that Smith has succeeded in reducing the formation of society to factors whose presence in man can be proven empirically, while

9. A. Smith, *The Theory of Moral Sentiments*, Edinburgh, 1813, pt. II, sec. III, ch. III, p. 243. [American edition: *The Theory of Moral Sentiments* (Indianapolis: Liberty Classics, 1976), p. 195.]

Kant can explain society only through an assumption of man's "inclination" to associate and a second inclination to disassociate, from the antagonism of which society emerges. How it does so is not elaborated.[10]

Every teleological view can be dressed in a theistic garb without any change in its scientific character. For instance, Darwin's doctrine of natural selection can easily be presented in such a way that the struggle for survival becomes a wise arrangement by the Creator for the development of species. And every teleological view reveals harmonies to us, that is, how that which stands at the end of the development process emerges from the acting forces. The fact that the conditions cooperate harmoniously only signifies that they lead to the effect we are to explain. If we desist from calling a given state of affairs "good," all tenets of the doctrine stay intact. The explanation of how a certain state "necessarily" had to result from given conditions that cannot be analyzed further, is independent of how we may value this state. The attacks on the thought of "preestablished harmony" do not touch the substance, merely the wording, of the utilitarian social theory.

Without change in substance, the social doctrine of Marxism, too, can be understood as one announcing a preestablished harmony. The dialectics of social reality necessarily lead the way from the primeval world to the goal, the socialistic paradise. The unsatisfactory part of this doctrine is its content; the wording again is unimportant.

The opponents of utilitarian social theory like to taunt it for its "rationalism." But every scientific explanation is rationalistic. Whatever the human mind cannot comprehend, the tools of science cannot conquer. This criticism often ignores the fact that liberal social theory does not explain formation and progress of social ties and institutions as consciously aimed human efforts toward the formation of societies, as the naive versions of the contract theory explain them. It views social organizations "as the unconsidered re-

10. See Kant, "Idee zu einer allgemeinen Geschichte in weltbürgerlicher Absicht" [Ideas on a general history from a cosmopolitan view], Collected Works, Insel ed., Leipzig, vol. I, p. 227 et seq.

sult of specific *individual* efforts of the members of society."[11]

The misunderstanding that prevails with regard to the harmony doctrine is repeated in a different form regarding property. We can either hold to the opinion that the private property order is the superior form of social organization—that is, we can be liberals—or we can believe that the public property order is superior—that is, we can be socialists. But he who adheres to the former embraces the doctrine that the private property order serves the interests of all members of society, not just those of owners.[12]

We proceed from the position that there are no insoluble conflicts of interest within the private property order, even to the recognition that warlike behavior becomes rarer as the scope and intensity of social association grows. Wars, foreign and domestic (revolutions, civil wars), are more likely to be avoided the closer the division of labor binds men. The belligerent creature, man, becomes industrial, the "hero" becomes a "trader." The democratic institutions serve to eliminate violent action within the state, as they seek to maintain or achieve agreement between the wills of those who govern and those who are governed.

In contrast to the utilitarians who believe that the private property order assures greater labor productivity, the older socialists were convinced that it was the public property system that could bring higher productivity, which necessitated the abolition of the private property order. We must distinguish this utilitarian socialism from the socialism that takes as its starting point a theistic or metaphysical social theory, and that demands a command system because it is

---

11. Menger, *Untersuchungen über die Methode der Sozialwissenschaften* [Inquiries into the methods of social sciences], Leipzig, 1883, p. 178. [English-language edition: *Problems of Economics and Sociology* (Urbana, Ill.: University of Illinois Press, 1963).] F. v. Wieser's critique of the rationalistic-utilitarian doctrine in general, and of Menger's formulation in particular, leaves its substance untouched (See Wieser, *Theorie der gesellschaftlichen Wirtschaft* [Theory of social economics], Tübingen, 1914, sec. I, p. 242 *et seq.*). Its significance lies in its distinction between leader and masses—probably under the influence of Tarde—and in its greater emphasis on the principle of heterogeneity of objectives—as Wundt called it.
12. See A. Smith, *op. cit.*, pt. IV, ch. I, p. 417 *et seq.* [American edition: p. 297 *et seq.*]

more suited to realize empirically unproven values which society is to adopt.

The socialism of Marx fundamentally differs from these two varieties of socialism, which he calls "utopian." To be sure, Marx also assumes that the socialistic method of production yields higher labor productivity than the private property order. But he denies that a solidarity of interest exists or has ever existed in society. A solidarity of interest, according to Marx, can exist only within each class. But a conflict of interest exists between the classes, which explains why the history of all societies has been a history of class wars.

Conflict is the moving force of social development to yet another group of social doctrines. For those doctrines the war of races and nations constitute the basic law of society.

The common error of both groups of warfare sociology is their disregard of any principle of association. They endeavor to show why there must be war between the classes, races, and nations. But they neglect to show why there is, or can be, peace and cooperation between the classes, races and nations. The reason for this negligence is not difficult to detect. It is impossible to demonstrate a principle of association that exists within a collective group only, and that is inoperative beyond it. If war and strife are the driving force of all social development, why should this be true for classes, races, and nations only, and not for war among all individuals? If we take this warfare sociology to its logical conclusion we arrive at no social doctrine at all, but at "a theory of unsociability."[13]

None of this could be understood in Germany, Hungary, and the Slavic countries because of a basic hostility toward all utilitarian thought right from the start. Because modern sociology is based on utilitarianism and the doctrine of the division of labor, it was rejected summarily. This is the main reason for the reluctance of German scholars to cope with sociology, and for the struggle they waged so tenaciously for decades against sociology as a science. Since so-

---

13. Barth, *Die Philosophie der Geschichte als Soziologie* [The philosophy of history as sociology], 3rd ed., Leipzig, 1922, p. 260.

ciology was not welcome, a substitute had to be found. Depending on their political position they adopted one of the two "theories of unsociability" which emphasized the warfare principle, and completely bypassed any search for a principle of association.

This scientific situation explains the success Marxian sociology was able to achieve in Germany and in the East. When compared with the doctrines of racial and national warfare it had the advantage of offering, at least for the distant future, a social order with a coherent principle of association. Its answer was ever so much more acceptable because it was optimistic and more satisfactory for some readers than those doctrines which offered nothing in history but a hopeless struggle of a noble race against a supremacy of inferior races. He who sought to go even further in his optimism and was less exacting scientifically, found the solution to the conflict not just in the socialistic paradise of the future, but already in the "social kingdom."

Marxism thus swayed German thought in sociology and philosophy of history.

Popular German sociology adopted, above all, the class concept that is so basic to Marxian sociology. Spann correctly observed: "Today, even so-called middle-class economists are using the term 'class' in such a way and in connection with such questions as are raised by the historical materialism of Marx."[14] Adoption of this concept was accompanied by the Marx and Engels characteristics of uncertainty, vagueness, and obscurity, further echoed by the Social-Democrat and Communist parties. During the thirty-five years between the publication of the *Communist Manifesto* and his death, Marx did not succeed in somehow defining the concept of class struggle more precisely. And it is significant that the posthumous manuscript of the third volume of *Das Kapital* halts abruptly at the very place that was to deal with classes. Since his death more than forty years have passed, and the class struggle has become the cornerstone of modern German sociology. And yet we con-

---

14. O. Spann, "Klasse und Stand" [Class and estate], *Handwörterbuch*, 4th ed., vol. V, p. 692.

117

tinue to await its scientific definition and delineation. No less vague are the concepts of class interests, class condition, and class war, and the ideas on the relationship between conditions, class interests, and class ideology.

For Marx and his parties, the interests of the individual classes are irreconcilably opposed to each other. Each class knows precisely what its class interests are and how to realize them. Therefore, there can only be warfare, or at best an armistice. The thought that some circumstances may call an end to the struggle before the socialistic bliss is realized, or that circumstances may moderate it, is rejected summarily. There is no greater entity that could encompass the classes and dissolve the class conflicts. The ideas of fatherland, nation, race, and humanity are mere disguises for the only real fact, which is the class conflict. However, popular sociology does not go so far. It could be as Marx describes it, but it need not be so, and above all, it should not be that way. Selfish class interests must be set aside in order to serve the interests of nation, fatherland, state. And the state, as a principle of reason above the classes, as realization of the idea of justice, must intervene and bring about a social condition in which the ownership class is prevented from exploiting the nonowners, so that the class struggle of proletarians against owners becomes superfluous.

With the doctrine of class warfare, German etatist sociologists adopted the most important part of the Marxian philosophy of history. To them, the British parliamentary system with all its democratic institutions, of which liberal doctrine is singing praises, are mere expressions of the class supremacy of the bourgeoisie. As the Germans interpret contemporary British history, the British state and its instutitions are more reprehensible for being capitalistic and plutocratic. The British concept of liberty is contrasted with the German concept. They view the great French revolution and the movements of the 1830s and 1840s as class movements of the bourgeoisie. The fact that the principalities prevailed over the 1848 rebels in Germany is hailed as most fortunate, as it paved the way for the social rule of the Hohenzollern kaisers standing above classes and parties. To German etatists and Marxists, the modern imperialism of the allied powers springs from the capitalistic propensity to expand. The etatists also adopted a good part of the Marxian superstructure theory when they depicted classical economics as a handmaiden of the class interests of entrepreneurs and the bourgeoisie. An example given above illustrates how this applied even to Schmoller.

It should be noted that no critical examination preceeded the adoption of the basic Marxian doctrines. The attention of etatists was directed primarily at blunting the Marxian attack on the state ideology and its political offshoots during Prussian leadership in Germany, and at rendering the Marxian doctrines useful for the ideas of state socialism and conservatism. Etatists did not see the Marxian problem as a scientific problem, but as a political, or at best, an economic problem. In politics they contented themselves with charging Marxism with exaggerations, and sought to demonstrate that there is yet another solution, indeed, a better solution: social reform. Their main attack on Marxism did not aim at its economic program, but at its political program: it placed class interests above national interests.

Only a few comprehended that the problems raised by Marxism were scientific in nature. Sombart was one of the first who as continuator, renovator, and reformer set out to reshape the Marxian doctrines. His new work, which afforded me the occasion for this essay, provides me with the opportunity to deal with him in detail.

Dependence on Marx is the special characteristic of German social sciences. Surely Marxism has left its traces as well on the social thinking of France, Great Britain, the United States, the Scandinavian countries, and the Netherlands. But the influence that emanated from Marxian doctrines was incomparably greater in Germany. The fact that the sociology of utilitarianism was generally rejected in Germany undoubtedly offers an explanation for this great influence.[15] In Italy also, the influence of Marxism was rather significant, although not so strong as in Germany. But in Eastern Europe, in Hungary, and in the Slavic countries, it

---

15. If in the United States the influence of the antiutilitarians (e.g., that of Veblen) should spread, Marxism, too, will spread with all its consequences.

was even greater than in Germany—that is, it was greater in countries that completely depended on German thought in spite of their political hostility. Marxism had swayed Russian social thought, that is, not only the thinking of the followers of the revolutionary parties openly fighting czarism, but also the imperial Russian universities. Altschul, the translator of Gelesnoff's *Fundamental Economics*, correctly observed in his preface to the German edition, "In no other country did Marx's economic doctrines invade university teaching so quickly and influence it so significantly as in Russia."[16] In its hatred of liberalism and democracy czarism itself paved the way for the Bolshevist ideology through its promotion of Marxism.

# 2.
# National (Anti-Marxian) Socialism

Marxian socialism is beckoning: "Class war, not national war!" It is proclaiming: "Never again [imperialistic] war." But it is adding in thought: "Civil war forever, revolution."

National socialism is beckoning: "National unity! Peace among classes!" And it is adding in thought: "War on the foreign enemy!"[17]

---

16. Gelesnoff, *Grundzüge der Volkswirtschaftslehre* [Fundamental economics], Leipzig, 1918, p. iii.

17. We must not search for ideas of national socialism just within the National Socialist Party, which is merely a part—in questions of party tactics an especially radical part—of the greater movement of national socialism that comprises all people's parties. The most eminent literary spokesmen for national socialism are Oswald Spengler and Othmar Spann. A short and very instructive summary of the ideas of national socialism is contained in the program of the Greater German People's Party of Austria written by Otto Conrad, *Richtlinien deutscher Politik. Programmatische Grundlagen der Grossdeutschen Volkspartei* [Guidelines for German policy. Program principles of the greater German people's party], Vienna, 1920.

These solutions distill the ideas which are dividing the German nation into two hostile camps.

The great political problem of Germany is the national one. It appears in three different forms: as the problem of the linguistically mixed territories at the borders of German settlement in Europe, as the problem of German emigration (a creation of German settlements overseas), and as the problem of foreign trade that must provide the material support for the German population.

Marxism did not see these problems at all. It could say only that in the socialistic paradise of the future there will be no national struggle. "National hatred is transformed class hatred," its holder is "the middle class," its beneficiary the "bourgeoisie," proclaim the party literati.[18] How could there be national conflicts after class distinctions and exploitation have been abolished?

The national problem is a world political problem, the greatest world problem in the foreseeable future. It concerns all nations, not just the German nation. During the eighteenth and nineteenth centuries, when the English and French formulated modern political doctrines, it had a different meaning for them than it has today. The first civilized country for which the national problem became important in its present form was Germany. It should have been the task of German political theory to deal with it and find a solution through practical politics. The British and French did not know all those problems of nationalism for which the formula of national self-determination does not suffice. German politics did face these problems for decades, and should have met the challenge by finding a solution. But German theory and practice could only proclaim the principle of force and struggle. Its application isolated the German nation from the world, and led to its defeat in the Great War.

Where the areas in which the German people settled meet with those occupied by the Danes, Lithuanians, Poles, Czechs, Hungarians, Croats, Slovaks, Italians, and French, the population borders are not clearly marked out. In wide

---

18. See O. Bauer, *Die Nationalitätenfrage und die Sozialdemokratie* [The nationality problem and social democracy], Vienna, 1907, pp. 263, 268.

121

sections the peoples are mixed, and individual linguistic islands, especially urban centers, reach far into foreign areas. Here the formula of "self-determination of nations" no longer suffices. For here are national minorities who fall under foreign rule if the majority principle determines political government. If the state is a liberal state under the rule of law, merely protecting the property and personal safety of its citizens, the alien rule is less palpable. It is felt more keenly the more society is governed, the more the state becomes a welfare state, the more etatism and socialism gain a footing.

For the German nation a violent solution to the problem is least satisfactory. If Germany, a nation surrounded by other nations in the heart of Europe, were to assault in accordance with this principle, it would invite a coalition of all its neighbors into a world-political constellation: enemies all around. In such a situation Germany could find only one ally: Russia, which is facing hostility by Poles, Lithuanians, Hungarians, and possibly Czechs, but nowhere stands in direct conflict with German interests. Since Bolshevist Russia, like Czarist Russia, only knows force in dealing with other nations, it is already seeking the friendship of German nationalism. German Anti-Marxism and Russian Super-Marxism are not too far apart. But various attempts at reconciling German Anti-Marxian nationalism with the Anti-Marxian nationalism of Fascist Italy must fail in dealing with South Tirol, just as a reconciliation of Hungarian chauvinism must fail in dealing with the West-Hungarian problem.

A violent solution to the question of border Germans would be less acceptable for the German nation itself than for its neighbors, even if there were prospects for its realization. In fact, Germany, even if victorious on all sides, would need to be prepared for war at any time, would have to brace itself for another war of submission through starvation, and would have to prepare its economy for such an eventuality. This would impose a burden which, in the long run, could not be borne without serious consequences.

The trade problem, which Germany needed to solve during the nineteenth century, grew from a worldwide shifting of production to areas with more favorable production conditions. If there had been complete freedom of movement, a part of the German population would have emigrated, for German agriculture and some branches of industry could no longer compete with newly opened, more fertile countries offering more favorable production conditions. For national political reasons Germany sought to prevent this emigration through tariff policies. We cannot elaborate here why this attempt was doomed to failure.[19]

The migration problem is the third form of the practical political problem for Germany. Germany lacks territory for its excess population. And again, the prewar theory of German nationalism discovered no better solution than violence through conquest of suitable territory.

In Europe, tens of millions of people live poorly who would do much better in America and Australia. The difference in the living conditions between a European and his descendants overseas continues to grow. European emigrants could find overseas what their native countries failed to offer: a place at the banquet of nature. But they are too late. The descendants of those who, one, two, or three generations ago chose the New World over Europe, do not welcome them. The organized laborers of the United States and the British Commonwealth countries permit no addition of new competitors. Their labor union movement is not aimed at employers, as the Marxian doctrine prescribes; they are waging their "class war" against European workers whose immigration would reduce the marginal productivity of labor, and thus wage rates. The labor unions of the Anglo-Saxon countries favored participation in the Great War in order to eliminate the last remnants of the liberal doctrine of free movement and migration of labor. This was their war objective, which they adhered to completely. Countless Germans living abroad were uprooted, deprived of their possessions and earnings, and "repatriated." Today, strict laws either prohibit or limit immigration not only to the

19. I sought to explain it in my book *Nation, Staat und Wirtschaft* [Nation, state, and economy], Vienna, 1919, p. 45 *et seq.*

United States, but even to important European areas. And the labor unions of the United States and Australia unhesitatingly would favor a new, more horrible and bloody world war if it should become necessary to defend the immigration restrictions against an aggressor, such as the Japanese or a rearmed Germany.

Here are insurmountable difficulties for the Marxian doctrines and the policy of the Communist International. Theorists sought to escape the difficulties by not mentioning them. It is characteristic that the copious prewar German literature on economic and social policy, which again and again dealt with the same matter in tiring detail, contains no work that could explain the policy of immigration restrictions. And abroad only a few writers dared touch a topic that obviously did not harmonize with the doctrine of the workers' class solidarity.[20] This silence, better than anything else, reveals the Marxian bias in social literature, especially German literature. When, finally, the international conventions of socialists could no longer escape dealing with this question, they skillfully circumvented it. Let us, for instance, read the minutes of the International Convention of Socialists in Stuttgart, in 1907. It adopted a lame resolution characterized by the recorder himself as rather "awkward and hard." But this should be blamed on circumstances. A socialistic convention is not held "to write novels. Hard realities are colliding, which finds expression in this hard and awkward resolution." (This is a euphemistic way of admitting that something is wrong with the harmonious thoughts of the international solidarity of workers.) The writer therefore recommends that "this resolution so painfully constructed on the middle of the road be adopted unanimously." But the Australian representative Kröner crisply declared, "The majority of the Australian Labor Party opposes the immigration of colored workers. As a socialist, I personally recognize the duty of international solidarity and hope that in time we shall succeed in winning

---

20. The most comprehensive treatment is given by Prato, *Il proteezionismo operaio*, Turin, 1910. (French translation by Bourgin, Paris, 1912.) The book remained almost unknown in Germany.

all nations of the world for the idea of socialism."[21] Translated from the Australian to English it means: Make as many resolutions as you please; we shall do as we please. Since the Labor Party has come to power, Australia, as is well known, has the strictest immigration laws against colored and white workers.

The nationalistic Anti-Marxists of Germany could perform a great service by solving the emigration problem. The German mind could develop a new doctrine of universal freedom and free movement that would evoke an echo with Italians, Scandinavians, Slavs, Chinese, and Japanese, and which in the long run no nation could resist. But no beginning has yet been made of what needs to be done, and surely nothing has been accomplished.

National Anti-Marxism proved to be unproductive in the very point on which its greatest emphasis must be placed: the problem of foreign policy. Its program for the integration of the German nation in the world economy and world policy does not basically differ from the precept of German policy in recent decades. In fact, it does not differ from recent policy more than any theoretical doctrine differs from the realities faced by the statesman who is kept from his intended course by his daily tasks. But a violent solution is even less applicable today than it was in prewar Germany. Even a victorious Germany would be powerless to face the real problems of the German nation. In the present state of world affairs, Germany could never prevail over the opposing national interests of other nations, that is, it could not acquire overseas territory for German settlement and open up favorable markets for German industry. Above all, it could never be safe from a resumption of the war by a new coalition of enemies.

National Anti-Marxism is failing as well in providing suitable German policy for pressing present problems. In their struggle against forced integration, the German minorities in foreign countries must demand the most compre-

---

21. *International Convention of Socialists at Stuttgart, August 18–24, 1907*, Berlin, 1907, p. 57–64.

hensive democracy because only self-government can protect them from losing their German identity. They must demand full economic freedom because every intervention in the hands of the foreign state becomes a means of discrimination against the German population.[22] But how can the German population in the border territories fight for democracy and economic freedom if the Reich itself conducts a contrary policy?

National Anti-Marxism has also failed on scientific grounds. The fact that the Marxian theories of value and distribution have lost their prestige is not the achievement of Anti-Marxism, but that of the Austrian School, especially Böhm-Bawerk's critique which the young friends of theoretical economics in Germany could no longer overlook. Surely, the attempts by some writers to confer prestige on Marx as a philosopher have little prospect for success, because, after all, philosophical knowledge in Germany has reached a level that makes scholars somewhat immune to the naivetés of the "philosophy" of Marx, Dietzgen, Vorländer, and Max Adler. However, in the field of sociology the categories and thoughts of Marxian materialism continue to spread. Here, Anti-Marxism could have solved an important task; but it was content with attacking those final conclusions of Marxism that appeared to be objectionable politically, without refuting its foundation and replacing it with a comprehensive doctrine. It had to fail, because for political reasons it sought to show that Marxism is animated by the spirit of the West, that it is an offspring of individualism—a concept alien to German character.

The very starting point is fallacious. We already mentioned that it is not permissible to contrast the universalistic (collectivistic) with the individualistic (nominalistic) systems of social doctrine and policy, as set forth by Dietzel and Pribram, and now advocated by Spann with his nationalis-

22. See the excellent discussions by F. Wolfrum, "Der Weg zur deutschen Freiheit" [The road to German freedom], *Freie Welt*, Gablonz, vol. IV, Booklet 95, and "Staatliche Kredithilfe" [Credit assistance by the state], *Freie Welt*, Booklet 99. In Czechoslovakia every government intervention serves to make the minorities Czech; in South Tirol and in Poland the Italians and Poles do not act any differently.

tic German Anti-Marxism. It is also erroneous to view Marxian socialism as the successor to the liberal democracy of the first half of the nineteenth century. The connection between the socialism of Marx and Lassalle and the early democratic program was rather superficial, and was discarded as serving no further purpose as soon as the Marxian parties came to power. Socialism is no improvement over liberalism; it is its enemy. It is illogical to deduce a similarity of the two from an opposition to both.

Marxism does not spring from Western thought. As mentioned above, it failed to find followers in Western countries because it could not overcome the utilitarian sociology. The greatest difference between German ideas and those of the West is the great influence of Marxian thought in Germany. And German thought will not be able to overcome Marxism until it sheds its hostility toward British, French, and American sociology. To be sure, it cannot just adopt the sociology of the West, but it must continue and build anew on its foundation.

# 3.
# Sombart as Marxist and Anti-Marxist

Werner Sombart himself proudly confessed that he gave a good part of his life to fight for Marx.[23] It was Sombart, not the wretched pedants of the ilk of Kautsky and Bernstein, who introduced Marx to German science and familiarized German thought with Marxist doctrines. Even the structure

23. See W. Sombart, *Das Lebenswerk von Karl Marx* [The life's work of Karl Marx], Jena, 1909, p. 3.

of Sombart's main work, *Modern Capitalism,* is Marxian. The problem Marx raised in *Das Kapital* and other writings is to be solved again, this time with the means of advanced knowledge. And as with Marx, theoretical analysis is to be combined with historical presentation. The starting point of his work is completely Marxian, but its findings are purported to go beyond Marx. Thus, he differs from the publications of party Marxists whose findings are rigidly circumscribed by party doctrine.

Sombart built his reputation as a Marxist and scholar in 1896 with his little book *Socialism and the Social Movement during the Nineteenth Century.* The booklet saw several editions, and each new edition gave evidence of the changes in Sombart's position on the problems of socialism and the social movement. The tenth edition, revised, is now available in two imposing volumes.[24] It is to demonstrate and justify his turning away from Marxism—but not from socialism. In fact, the two volumes do not deal with socialism as such, but rather with "proletarian socialism," with "Marxism."

Sombart deals only with a history and critique of Marxian socialism. He avoids revealing his own social doctrine, which he briefly touches upon in a few places. With visible satisfaction he speaks of the old associations of the Middle Ages—church, town, village, clan, family, vocation— "which contained the individual, warmed him, and protected him like a fruit in its peel." And with visible horror he speaks of that "process of disintegration which shattered the world of faith and replaced it with knowledge."[25] The ideology of proletarian socialism is seen as an expression of this disintegration process. And between the lines he is reproaching proletarian socialism for its express preference for modern industrialism. "Whatever socialistic critique may have raised against capitalism, it never objected on grounds that capitalism has blessed us with railroads and factories, steel furnaces and machines, telegraph wires and motorcy-

24. W. Sombart, *Der proletarische Sozialismus, Marxismus* [Proletarian socialism, Marxism], 10th ed., rev., of *Sozialismus und soziale Bewegung* [Socialism and social movement], Jena, 1924; vol. I, *The Doctrine,* vol. II, *The Movement.*
25. *Ibid.,* vol. I, p. 31.

cles, record players and airplanes, movie theatres and power centers, cast iron and aniline colors." Proletarianism, according to Sombart, merely rejects the social form, not the gist of modern civilization. And with clear emphasis on his own position he confronts proletarian socialism with the "preproletarian chimera," with its "bucolic" flavor which always praised agriculture as the most noble vocation and looked upon agrarian culture as its ideal.[26]

This infatuation with agrarian society and the Middle Ages deserves our comment. We meet it again and again in the literature of nationalistic Anti-Marxism, with variations by individual authors. For Spann, the leader of this movement, the ideal was a return to the Middle Ages.[27]

He who depicts the social institutions and economic organizations of the Middle Ages as models for the German people, should be aware that a bucolic Germany could support only a fraction of the present population even with the greatest curtailment of expectations. Every proposal that would reduce the productivity of labor diminishes the supportable population, and, through the deterioration of the apparatus of production, would weaken the national defenses that are so important from a nationalistic point of view. Nor can nationalism seek a solution of the German problem in a return to an agrarian society. The incompatibility of the bucolic ideals with a powerful development of national forces may explain the dark pessimism of the "doom theories" that are springing up in various forms.

If it should be true that the particular ethos of the German nation is demanding a return to production methods that lead to lower labor productivity, and that, inversely, the Western nations, the Latin nations of the South, and Slavic nations in the East think differently and apply production methods that assure higher labor productivity, the danger is real that the more numerous and productive enemies will overpower the German nation. Will the philosophers of the victors not conclude then that it was lack of adaptability that

---

26. *Ibid.*, vol. I, p. 257 *et seq.*
27. See O. Spann, *op. cit.*, p. 298 *et seq.*

prevented the Germans from making use of their capitalistic methods of production? Will they not look upon the German mentality as being too poor and unfit for keeping its spiritual equilibrium in the presence of modern technological achievements?

Indeed, it is a gross materialistic feature of otherwise idealistic writers who believe that some externalities of life are blocking the way to inner growth and the development of inner strength. He who does not know how to safeguard his equilibrium when surrounded by motorcycles and telephones will not find it in the jungle or desert. That is, he will not find the strength to overcome the nonessential with the essential. Man must be able to safeguard himself whereever he lives and whatever the circumstances should be. It is a sickly weakness of nerves that urges one to seek harmonious personality growth in past ages and remote places.

Sombart, as already mentioned, reveals his social ideal only between the lines. He cannot be criticized for this. But we must fault him for not offering a precise definition of the concept of socialism in a book that seeks to present and analyze a certain kind of socialism. His discussion of socialistic ideology, which introduces the work, is its weakest part. Sombart rejects the thought that socialism is a social order based on public property in the means of production. Obviously, the concept of socialism would have to be a social one, or of the social sciences, he argues, and could not be from a special field of social life, such as the economy. The emotions accompanying the controversy over socialism reveal that the term socialism must comprise yet deeper problems than "economic technology."[28] But the definition Sombart then offers must finally return—although with ambiguity—to the only relevant characteristic of socialism. After lengthy discussions he arrives at the conclusion that the idea of socialism always comprises the following components:

1. The ideal of a rational condition of society is to be contrasted with a historical condition that is irra-

---

28. See Sombart, *Sozialismus und soziale Bewegung, op. cit.*, vol. I, p. 5 *et seq.*

tional: that is, an evaluation of social conditions as perfect or less perfect. Certain features of the ideal that are common to all kinds of socialism relate to the anti-capitalistic essence of socialism: *socialism obviously must reject an economy for profit* because of its irrational objectives that spring from its guiding principle. As money symbolizes the capitalistic economy for profit, it is as such a favorite target of socialistic critique. All evil of this world comes from the struggle over the ring of the Nibelungs; therefore, socialism wants to return the gold to the Rhine. *In the manner socialism opposes the "free" economy it also opposes its foundation: "free," i.e., private, property and the "free," i.e., labor, contract.* It gives rise to exploitation, the worst blemish of social life, the eradication of which is an essential program for all kinds of socialism.

2. Valuation of social conditions and adoption of a rational ideal necessarily correspond to the recognition of moral freedom, the freedom to strive for a realm of objectives with one's own strength, and the faith in the possibility of its realization.

3. Ideal and freedom inevitably give birth to an aspiration for realizing the ideal, a movement, born in freedom, from the historically given to the rationally desired. But every confession of socialism means a renunciation of motive power, that is, from the viewpoint of the individual it means: obligation, sacrifice, limitation of the particular.[29]

There can be only one reason why Sombart chooses this detour, instead of retaining the proven and only viable definition of socialism: his aversion toward dealing with the genuine economic problems of socialism, an aversion that permeates his whole work and constitutes its greatest deficiency. The fact that Sombart never raises the question of whether or not a socialistic order is possible and realizable is even more serious than his renunciation of a clear defini-

---

29. Emphasis added. *Ibid.*, vol. I, p. 12 *et seq.*

tion of socialism. For only this question can provide the foundation for an understanding of socialism and the socialistic movement.

But Sombart does not want to deal with socialism in general; he wants to analyze proletarian socialism, or Marxism. However, his definition is unsatisfactory even for proletarian socialism which, according to Sombart,

> is merely an intellectual sediment of the modern social movement as I have defined it since the first edition of this book. Socialism and social movement are . . . the realization of that future social order that is adjusted to the interests of the proletariat, or the attempt at its realization. Socialism seeks its realization in the world of thought, the socialistic movement in the world of reality. All theoretical efforts toward revealing the desired goal to the aspiring proletariat, toward calling it to arms, organizing for battle, and showing the road on which the goal can be reached, all comprise what we call modern socialism.[30]

One thing is noticeable in this definition: it is Marxian. It is no coincidence that Sombart deems it proper to adopt this definition unchanged from his first edition, from the time when, by his own admission, he was still walking in the footsteps of Marx. It contains an important element from the Marxian world of thought: socialism suits the interests of the proletariat. This is a specific Marxian thought that is meaningful only within the framework of the whole Marxian structure. "Utopian" socialism of the pre-Marxian era and the state socialism in recent decades acted, not in the interests of one class but on behalf of all classes and the collective whole. Marxism introduced the two axioms that society is divided into classes whose interests conflict irreconcilably, and that the interests of the proletariat—realizable through class war only—are demanding nationalization of

---

30. *Ibid.*, vol. I, p. 19 *et seq.*

the means of production, in accordance with their own interests and contrary to those of the other classes.

This very thought returns in various places in the book. At one place Sombart observes that very few influential Marxian writers come from the proletariat "and therefore are only interested parties."[31] And then point-blank: "The proletariat belongs to the system of capitalism; the inevitability of hostility toward capitalists springs from the class conditions of the proletariat. This hostility assumes certain forms in the social movement: labor unions, socialistic parties, strikes, etc."[32] It cannot be denied that the materialistic philosophy of history is visible here in full display. To be sure, Sombart does not draw the conclusion which Marx logically drew in this case: that socialism is coming with the inevitability of natural law.[33] According to Sombart, the "science of capitalism" founded by Marx introduced "the idea of the regularity of economic life in our era." It reveals "that the realization of any particular socialistic demand depends on very real, objective conditions and that, therefore, socialism may not always be realizable." Marx thus created "scientifically" the thought of resignation which logically leads from socialism to social reform.[34] We need not dwell further on the question of whether Sombart's conclusion is the one that must logically be drawn from the doctrines of Marx, or whether the opinion of Lenin and Trotsky is the logical one. It is decisive that Sombart unconsciously continues to stand on the scientific ground of Marxism. (Sombart drew the reform conclusion in his earlier writings; this is the "Sombartism" of which the orthodox Marxists speak with derogatory gestures, as they always do when something displeases them.)

Wherever Sombart seeks to describe capitalism he does so in the framework of Marx and Engels, often in their own words.[35]

---

31. *Ibid.*, vol. I, p. 75.
32. *Ibid.*, vol. II, p. 261.
33. *Ibid.*, vol. I, p. 305.
34. *Ibid.*, vol. I, p. 304.
35. *Ibid.*, vol. I, p. 32 *et seq.*

Such are the characteristics of Sombart's position on Marxism: while he does not embrace the founder's naively materialistic version of socialism today, Sombart builds his more refined socialistic doctrines on the foundation of Marxism. And he draws practical conclusions other than those of orthodox Marxists. In fact, he does not oppose socialism in any form.

Sombart reproaches Marx not for his doctrine of class warfare, but for its politicalization and the final conclusion Marx draws from the doctrine: the inevitability of the proletarian victory.[36] In other words, Sombart does not say that the Marxian separation of classes does not exist, or that the properly understood interests of the various layers of population working in a division of labor do not conflict with each other, but are harmonious. But he says: Ethics must overcome the conflict of class interests. Besides the class principle "there are other social principles—namely those of idealistic nature." But Marxism makes the class concept absolute.[37] Sombart apparently believes that man must submerge his class interests and give precedence to higher interests, to national interests. He reproaches the Marxists for not thinking in terms of fatherland, for conducting world policies, for advocating class warfare in domestic policies, and for remaining pacifistic and antinationalistic in foreign policies.

Sombart completely ignores the scientific criticism of the Marxian class doctrine. This is necessary because he wants to ignore utilitarianism and economic theory and because, in the final analysis, he considers Marxism as the true science of capitalism. According to Sombart, "Marx founded . . . the science of capitalism."[38] Long ago this science "demonstrated conclusively, that this economic order contains the essence of the destruction and dissolution of civilization. Karl Marx was the greatest, if not the first, harbinger of this knowledge."[39] In order to escape the conclusions that

---

36. *Ibid.*, vol. I, p. 368 *et seq.*
37. *Ibid.*, vol. I, p. 356.
38. *Ibid.*, vol. I, p. 304.
39. W. Sombart, "Das Finstere Zeitalter" [The dark age], *Neue Freie Presse* [New free press], Dec. 25, 1924.

must be drawn from Marx's theories, Sombart knows nothing better than to appeal to God and eternal values.

Sombart is quite right when he professes that it is not the function of science to provide a "value critique, that is, to reveal the inferiority of individual words, analyses, and principles of proletarian socialism." But he is mistaken when he declares that scientific critique is "but a discovery of relationships and their significance, relationships not only between the various doctrines and corresponding political demands, but also between the content of the whole system and the basic questions of intellectual civilization and human fate."[40] That is the position of historicism which is content with pursuing relationships among scientific theories and between scientific theories and metaphysical systems of thought, but abstains from developing scientific theories of its own. A sociological theory, which Marxism represents in spite of its shortcomings, can be analyzed only by examining its usefulness for an explanation of social phenomena. And it can be replaced only with a theory that is more satisfactory.[41]

It could not be otherwise. Sombart's critique of proletarian socialism rests on a subjective value judgment of what he considers the "basic values" of the proletariat. Here, world view meets world view, metaphysics confronts metaphysics. It is confession, not perception, and has no bearing on science. Of course, there are many readers who appreciate Sombart's work for this very reason. It does not limit itself to the narrow field of scientific labor, but offers metaphysical syntheses. It is not mere scientific research, but the presentation of material permeated with the spirit and personality of the man and thinker, Sombart. This is what gives the book its character and significance. In the end it convinces only those readers who already share Sombart's view.

Sombart does not attempt a critique of the means by which socialism proposes to attain its ends. And yet, any

---

40. *Ibid.*
41. I cannot here go into the details of a critique of the class doctrine; I must refer the reader to my *Gemeinwirtschaft,* Jena, 1922, p. 265–352. [English-language edition: *Socialism* (London: Jonathan Cape, 1936), p. 281–358.]

scientific analysis of socialism must first examine the thesis of the higher productivity of socialistic production, and then question whether or not a socialistic mode of production is possible at all. Nor does Sombart's criticism more than touch upon the problem of the inevitability of socialism.

Sombart's book is a special literary phenomenon. It frequently happens that in a scholar's lifetime he changes his opinion and in a new book advocates what he opposed earlier. But it was always a new book that revealed the intellectual change, as, for instance, Plato's *Laws* which followed his *Republic*. It is very rare, however, that an author reveals his lifelong struggle with one problem in ever new revisions of the same work, as does Sombart. Therefore, we must not conclude that the present edition contains the last version of his statement on socialism. Many years of labor lie ahead, new editions of *Socialism* will be needed not only because previous editions are out of print, but because Sombart has not yet completed his work on the problems of socialism. The book in its present form merely represents a stage in Sombart's struggle with Marxism. He has not yet freed himself as much as he thinks he has. A great deal of intellectual work remains to be done.

Sombart's inner struggle with the problems of Marxism is symptomatic of the thinking of many German scholars. Each edition of the book reflects rather well what the intellectual leaders of Germany have been thinking of this problem. The changes in his opinion mirror the changes in the opinion of German intellectuals who have followed his leadership for a generation.

# 4.
# Anti-Marxism and Science

Anti-Marxism fully subscribes to Marxism's hostility towards capitalism. And it resents Marxism's political program, especially its presumed internationalism and pacifism. But resentment does not lend itself to scientific work, or even to politics. At best it lends itself to demagoguery.

But for every scientific thinker the objectionable point of Marxism is its theory, which seems to cause no offense to the Anti-Marxist. We have seen how Sombart continues to appreciate Marx as a man of science. The Anti-Marxist merely objects to the political symptoms of the Marxian system, not to its scientific content. He regrets the harm done by Marxian policies to the German people, but is blind to the harm done to German intellectual life by the platitudes and deficiencies of Marxian problems and solutions. Above all, he fails to perceive that political and economic troubles are consequences of this intellectual calamity. He does not appreciate the importance of science for everyday living, and, under the influence of Marxism, believes that "real" power instead of ideas is shaping history.

We can completely agree with Anti-Marxism that the recovery of Germany must begin with overcoming Marxism. But this overcoming, if it is to be permanent, must be the work of science, not of a political movement that is guided by resentment. German science must free itself of the bonds of Marxism by putting behind it the historicism which for decades has kept it intellectually impotent. It must shed its fear of theory in economics and sociology and get acquainted with the theoretical achievements (even those by Germany) attained during the last generation.

Carl Menger's statements of more than forty years ago on

137

modern German economic literature are still valid today and apply to all the social sciences: "Scarcely noticed abroad, and barely understandable abroad on account of its peculiar tendencies, German economics for decades has remained untouched by serious opponents. With unflinching confidence in its own methods it often has lacked serious self-criticism. He who pursued another direction in Germany was ignored, not refuted."[42] Only a thorough study of the works of German and foreign sociology differing from etatism and historicism could help to extricate it from the deadlock of prevailing doctrine in Germany. German science would not be the only beneficiary. Great problems await their solution that cannot be achieved without German cooperation. Again in the words of Menger: "All great civilized nations have their particular mission in the unfolding of science. Each aberration of a sizeable number of scholars of one nation leaves a gap in the development of scientific knowledge. Economics, too, cannot do without the singleminded cooperation of the German mind."[43]

Above all, German science must make a proper assessment of the importance of Marxism. It is true, the Marxists and Anti-Marxists greatly overestimate Marxism as a scientific system. But also those who deny Marx as the first harbinger of the substance of the Marxian doctrine raise no objection against the validity of the doctrine itself. Only he who can see the world without Marxian blinders may approach the great problems of sociology. Only when German science has freed itself from the Marxian errors in which it is enmeshed today, then, and only then, will the power of Marxist slogans disappear from political life.

---

42. C. Menger, *op. cit.*, p. xx *et seq.*
43. *Ibid.*, p. xxi.

# THEORY OF PRICE CONTROLS[1]

# 1.
# Introduction

The knowledge that the constellation of the market determines prices precisely, or at least within narrow limits, is relatively new. Some earlier writers may have had a dim notion of it, but only the Physiocrats and the classical economists elaborated a system of exchange and market relations. The science of catallactics thus replaced the indeterminism of theory, which explained prices from the demands of sellers, and saw no price limits other than their fairness.

He who believes the formation of prices to be arbitrary easily arrives at the demand that they should be fixed by external regulation. If the conscience of the seller is lacking, if without fear of the wrath of God he demands more than is "fair," a worldly authority must intervene in order to help justice prevail. And minimum prices must be imposed for certain commodities and services over which buyers are believed, not quite logically, to have the power to force devia-

---

1. *Handwörterbuch der Staatswissenschaften* [Handbook of social sciences], 4th ed., vol. VI, 1923.

tions from the just price. Government is called upon to create order because disorder and arbitrariness prevail.

The practical doctrine based on the knowledge of scientific economics and sociology—liberalism—rejects all intervention as superfluous, useless, and harmful. It is superfluous because built-in forces are at work that limit the arbitrariness of the exchanging parties. It is useless because the government objective of lower prices cannot be achieved by controls. And it is harmful because it deters production and consumption from those uses that, from the consumer's viewpoint, are most important. At times liberalism has called government intervention impossible. Of course, government can issue orders that regulate prices and punish the violators. Therefore, it would have been more appropriate for liberalism not to call price controls impossible, but rather unsuitable, that is, running counter to the intentions of their advocates. The following discussion will demonstrate this unsuitability.

Liberalism was soon replaced by socialism, which seeks to replace private property in the means of production with public property. Socialism as such need not reject the price knowledge of science; it is conceivable that it could recognize its usefulness for an understanding of market phenomena in its own economic order. If it were to do that, it would have to conclude that government and other interference with prices is as superfluous, useless, and harmful as liberalism says it is. In fact, the doctrines of Marxism contain, besides quite incompatible principles and demands, the beginnings of this perception; this is clearly visible in the skepticism toward the belief that wage rates can be raised by labor-union tactics, and in the rejection of all methods Marx calls "bourgeois." But in the world of Marxian reality etatism is dominant. In theory etatism is the doctrine of state omnipotence, and in practice, it is the government policy to manage all worldly matters through orders and prohibitions. The social ideal of etatism is a special kind of socialism, such as state socialism or, under certain conditions, military or religious socialism. On the surface the social ideal of etatism does not differ from the social order of capitalism. Etatism does not seek to overthrow the traditional legal order and formally convert all private property in production to public property. Only the largest enterprises in industry, mining, and transportation are to be nationalized. In agriculture, and in medium- and small-scale production, private property is to be preserved formally. But in substance all enterprises are to become government operations. Under this practice, the owners will keep their names and trademarks on the property and the right to an "appropriate" income or one "befitting their ranks." Every business becomes an office and every occupation a civil service. There is no room for entrepreneurial independence in any of the varieties of state socialism. Prices are set by government, and government determines what is to be produced, how it is to be produced, and in what quantities. There is no speculation, no "extraordinary" profits, no losses. There is no innovation, except for that ordered by government. Government guides and supervises everything.

It is one of the peculiarities of etatist doctrine that it can envision man's social life only in terms of its special socialistic ideal. The outer similarity between the "social state" it extols and the social order based on private property in production causes it to overlook the essential difference that separates them. To the etatist, any dissimilarity of the two social orders is merely a temporary irregularity and a punishable violation of government orders. The state has slackened the reins, which it must pull short again, and everything will be in the best of order. The fact that man's social life is subject to certain conditions, to regularity like that of nature, is a concept that is alien to an etatist. To him, everything is power, which he views in a grossly materialistic light.

Although etatism did not succeed in supplanting the other socialistic ideals with its own ideal, it has defeated all other branches of socialism in practical policy. In spite of their diverging opinions and objectives all socialistic groups today seek to influence market prices through outside intervention and force.

141

The theory of price controls must investigate the effects of government interference with market prices in the private property order. It is not its task to analyze price controls in a socialistic order that preserves private property by form and outward appearance, and uses price controls to direct production and consumption. In this case the controls have only technical significance, and remain without influence on the nature of the issue. And they alone do not constitute the difference between the socialistic society that uses them and those socialistic societies that are organized along different lines.

The importance of the theory of price controls becomes evident in the contention that there is yet a third social order besides the private property order and one built on public property, an order that retains private property in the means of production, but is "regulated" through government intervention. The Socialists of the Chair and the Solidarists, together with a great many statesmen and powerful political parties, continue to hold to this belief. On the one hand, it plays a role in the interpretation of economic history during the Middle Ages, and on the other hand, it constitutes the theoretic foundation for modern interventionism.

# 2.
# Price Controls

*Sanctioning Controls.* We may call those controls "sanctioning" that set prices so close to those the unhampered market would set that only insignificant consequences can ensue. Such controls merely pursue a limited task and do not achieve great economic objectives through interference with market forces. Government may simply accept the market prices and sanction them with its intervention. The case is similar when government imposes price ceilings that lie above the market prices, and minimum prices that lie below them. The case is slightly different when government imposes controls in order to force a monopolist to charge competitive prices instead of higher monopolistic prices. If government creates monopolies or limits the number of competitors, thereby promoting monopolistic agreements, it must, without question, resort to price controls if it does not want to force consumers to pay monopolistic prices. In none of these cases is the result of government intervention a deviation of price from that of the unhampered market.

The situation is somewhat different when a government regulation deprives a seller of the opportunity, under certain conditions, to demand and obtain a price that is higher than that he can normally obtain. If, for instance, government fixed rates for taxicabs, cabbies would be prevented from exploiting those cases in which passengers are willing to pay more than normal rates. The affluent tourist who, late at night and in bad weather, arrives at a strange railroad station, accompanied by small children and loaded with many pieces of luggage, will gladly pay a much higher fare to get to a remote hotel if he must compete with others for the few or perhaps only taxicab offering a ride. With extraordinary gains from exceptional opportunities, the cabbies would be able, when business is poor, to charge lower rates in order to increase the demand for their services. Government intervention thus eliminates the difference between the fare at times of great demand and those of weak demand, and establishes an average rate. Now, if government fixes rates that are even lower than this ideal average price, we have genuine price control, to which I shall return shortly.

The case is similar where government does not set prices directly, but forces the seller, such as a restaurateur, to post his prices. This, too, has the effect that the seller is prevented from exploiting extraordinary situations in which he could obtain a higher price from individual buyers. He must take account of this limitation; if he is prevented from charging more under favorable conditions, he will find it difficult to charge less under unfavorable conditions.

Other price controls are to prevent windfall profits that might be reaped under extraordinary conditions. If a city power company for any reason should be prevented from generating power for a few days, candle prices would soar, and merchants with candle supplies would reap extraordinary profits. Now government intervenes and sets a price ceiling for candles, at the same time forcing the sale of candles as long as the supply lasts. This has no permanent effect on the candle supply inasmuch as the power failure is quickly corrected. Only insofar as merchants and producers, having such failures in mind, calculate prices and candle inventory does government intervention have future consequences. If the merchants must anticipate that under similar conditions government will again intervene, the price charged under normal conditions will rise and the incentive for larger inventories will be reduced.

*Genuine Controls.* We may call those price controls "genuine" that set prices differing from those the unhampered market would set. If government seeks to fix a price higher than the market price, it usually resorts to minimum prices. If government seeks to fix a price lower than the market price it usually imposes price ceilings.

Let us first consider the *ceiling*, or *maximum*, price. The natural price that would emerge in an unhampered market corresponds to an equilibrium of all prices. At that point price and cost coincide. Now, if a government order necessitates a readjustment, if the sellers are forced to sell their goods at lower prices, the proceeds fall below costs. Therefore, the sellers will abstain from selling—except for merchandise that quickly spoils or otherwise loses in value— and hold on to their goods in the hope that the government regulation will soon be lifted. But the potential buyers will be unable to buy the desired goods. If possible, they now may buy some substitute they would not have otherwise bought. (It should also be noted that the prices of these substitute goods must rise on account of the greater demand.) But it was never the intention of government to bring about

144

these effects. It wanted the buyers to enjoy the goods at lower prices, not to deprive them of the opportunity to buy the goods at all. Therefore, government tends to supplement the price ceiling with an order to sell all goods at this price as long as the supply lasts. At this point price controls encounter their greatest difficulty. The market interaction brings about a price at which demand and supply tend to coincide. The number of potential buyers willing to pay the market price is large enough for the whole market supply to be sold. If government lowers the price below that which the unhampered market would set, the same quantity of goods faces a greater number of potential buyers who are willing to pay the lower official price. Supply and demand no longer coincide; demand exceeds supply, and the market mechanism, which tends to bring supply and demand together through changes in price, no longer functions.

Mere coincidence now eliminates as many buyers as the given supply cannot accommodate. Perhaps those buyers who come first or have personal connections with the sellers will get the goods. The recent war with its many attempts at price controls provided examples of both. At the official price, goods could be bought either by a friend of the seller or by an early bird in the "polonaise." But government cannot be content with this selection of buyers. It wants everyone to have the goods at lower prices, and would like to avoid situations in which people cannot get any goods for their money. Therefore, it must go beyond the order to sell; it must resort to rationing. The quantity of merchandise coming to the market is no longer left to the discretion of sellers and buyers. Government now distributes the available supply and gives everyone at the official price what he is entitled to under the ration regulation.

But government cannot even stop here. The intervention mentioned so far concerns only the available supply. When that is exhausted the empty inventories will not be replenished because production no longer covers its costs. If government wants to secure a supply for consumers it must pronounce an obligation to produce. If necessary, it must fix the prices of raw materials and semimanufactured products, and eventually also wage rates, and force businessmen and workers to produce and labor at these prices.

It can thus be readily seen that it is inconceivable to resort to price controls as an isolated intervention in the private property order. Government is unable to achieve the desired result, and therefore finds it necessary to proceed step by step from the isolated pricing order to comprehensive control over labor, the means of production, what is produced, how it is produced, and how it is distributed. Isolated intervention in the market operation merely disrupts the service to consumers, and forces them to seek substitutes for those items they deem most important; it thus fails to achieve the very result government meant to achieve. The history of war socialism has clearly illustrated this. Governments seeking to interfere with market operations found it necessary, step by step, to proceed from the original isolated price interference to complete socialization of production. Government would have had to proceed ever faster if its price regulations had been observed more faithfully, and if black markets had not circumvented the regulations. The fact that government did not take the final step, the nationalization of the whole apparatus of production, was due to the early end of the war, which brought an end to the war economy. He who observes a war economy is clearly aware of the phases mentioned above: at first price control, then forced sales, then rationing, then regulation of production and distribution, and, finally, attempts at central planning of all production and distribution.

Price controls have played an especially important role in the history of coin debasement and inflationary policy. Again and again, governments have tried to enforce old prices in spite of coin debasement and expansion of circulating money. They did so again in the most recent and greatest of all inflation periods, during the World War. On the very day printing presses were put into the service of government finance, rising prices were fought with criminal law. Let us assume that this at first succeeded. And let us disregard the fact that the supply of goods was reduced by the war, which affected the exchange ratio between economic goods and money. Let us further ignore increased demand for money due to delayed money delivery or clearing system limitations and other restrictions. We merely wish to analyze the consequences of a policy that aims at stabilizing prices while the quantity of money is enlarged. The expansion of money creates new demand that did not exist before, "new purchasing power," as it is called. When the new buyers compete with those already in the market, and prices are not permitted to rise, only a part of demand can be satisfied. There are potential buyers who are willing to pay the price, but cannot find a supply. Government, which is circulating the newly created money, is seeking thereby to redirect commodities and services from previous uses to more desirable uses. It wants to buy them, not to commandeer them, which it certainly could do. Its intent is that money, only money, shall buy everything, and that potential buyers shall not be frustrated in their search for economic goods. After all, government itself wants to buy, it wants to use the market, not destroy it.

The official price is destroying the market on which commodities and services are exchanged for money. Wherever possible, the exchange continues in other ways. For instance, people resort to barter transactions, that is, to exchange without the interaction of money. Government, which is ill-prepared for such transactions because it owns no exchangeable goods, cannot approve of such a development. It is coming to the market with money only, and therefore is hoping that the purchasing power of the monetary unit is not further reduced by the money holders' inability to get the goods they want with their money. As a buyer of commodities and services itself, government cannot adhere to the principle that the old prices must not be exceeded. In short, government as issuer of new money cannot escape the consequences described by the quantity theory.

If government imposes a price higher than that determined by the unhampered market, and prohibits the sale at lower prices (minimum prices), demand must decline. At the lower market price supply and demand coincide. At the official higher price demand tends to trail supply, and some goods brought to the market cannot find a buyer. As government imposed the minimum price in order to assure the sellers profitable sales, the result was unintended by government. Therefore, it must resort to other means, which again, step by step, must lead to complete government control over the means of production.

Especially significant are those minimum prices that set wage rates (minimum wages). Such rates may be set either directly by government or indirectly by promoting labor union policies that aim at establishing minimum wages. When, through strikes or threats of strikes, labor unions enforce a wage rate that is higher than that determined by the unhampered market, they can do so only with the assistance of government. The strike is made effective by denying the protection of the law and administration to workers willing to work. In fact, it is irrelevant for our analysis whether the apparatus of coercion imposing the controls is the "legitimate" state apparatus or a sanctioned apparatus with public power. If a minimum wage that exceeds the unhampered market rate is imposed on a particular industry, its costs of production are raised, the price of the final product must rise, and correspondingly, sales must decline. Workers lose their jobs, which depresses wages in other industries. Up to this point we may agree with the wage fund theory on the effects of nonmarket wage boosts. That which the workers in one industry are gaining is lost by the workers in other industries. In order to avoid such consequences, the imposition of minimum wages must be accompanied by the prohibition to dismiss workers. The prohibition in turn reduces the industry's rate of return because unneeded workers must be paid, or they are used and paid in full production while their output is sold at a loss. Industrial activity then tends to decline. If this, too, is to be prevented, government must intervene again with new regulations.

If the minimum wage is not limited to a few industries, but is imposed on all industries of an isolated economy, or on the world economy, the rise in product prices caused by it cannot lead to a reduction in consumption.[2] The higher wages raise the workers' spending power. They can now buy the higher-priced products coming to the market. (To be sure, there may be shifting within the industries.) If entrepreneurs and capitalists do not want to consume their capital they must limit their consumption since their money income has not risen and they are unable to pay the higher prices. To the extent of this reduction in consumption, the general wage boost has given the workers a share of entrepreneurial profits and capital income. The workers' real raise is visible in that prices do not rise by the full amount of the wage boost because of the entrepreneurs' and capitalists' cutback in consumption. That is, the rise in consumer prices is less than that of wages. But it is well known that even if all property income were divided among the workers, their individual incomes would rise very little, which should dispel any illusion about such a reduction in property income. But if we were to assume that the wage boost and rise in prices should allocate a large part, if not all, of the real income of entrepreneurs and capitalists to workers, we must bear in mind that the former want to live and will therefore consume their capital for lack of entrepreneurial income. Elimination of capital income through coercive wage boosts thus merely leads to capital consumption, and thereby to continuous reduction in national income. (By the way, every attempt at abolishing capital income must have the same consequence unless it is achieved through all-round nationalization of production and consumption.) If again government seeks to avoid these undesirable effects, no alternative is left, from the etatist point of view, but to seize control over the means of production from the owners.

Our discussion applies only to those price controls that endeavor to set prices differing from those of the unhampered market. If the controls should seek to undercut monopolistic prices, the consequences are quite different. Government then may effectively intervene anywhere

---

2. We are ignoring the monetary forces' exerting their influence on prices.

in the range between the higher monopolistic price and the lower competitive price. Under certain conditions price controls may deprive a monopolist of specific monopolistic gains. Let us assume, for instance, that in an isolated economy a sugar cartel is holding sugar prices above those the unhampered market would set. Government could then impose a minimum price for sugar beets that is higher than the unhampered market price. But the effects of price controls could not develop as long as the intervention merely absorbs the specific monopoly gain of the sugar monopolist. Only when the beet price is set so high that sugar production becomes unprofitable even at the monopolistic price, forcing the sugar monopoly to raise prices and curtail production in line with shrinking demand, will the price control effects take place.

# 3.
# The Significance of the Theory of Price Control for the Theory of Social Organization

The most important theoretical knowledge gained from a basic analysis of the effects of price controls is this: the effect of intervention is the very opposite of what it was meant to achieve. If government is to avoid the undesirable consequences it cannot stop with just market interference. Step by step it must continue until it finally seizes control over production from the entrepreneurs and capitalists. It is unimportant, then, how it regulates the distribution of income, whether or not it grants a preferred income position to entrepreneurs and capitalists. It is important, however, that government cannot be satisfied with a single intervention, but is driven on to nationalize the means of production. This ultimate effect refutes the notion that there is a middle form of organization, the "regulated" economy, between the private property order and the public property order. In the former only the play of market forces can determine prices. If government prevents this play in any way, production loses its meaning and becomes chaotic. Finally, government must assume control in order to avoid the chaos it created.

Thus, we must agree with the classical liberals and some older socialists who believed it impossible in the private property order to eliminate the market influence on prices, and thereby on production and distribution, by decreeing prices that differ from market prices. For them it was no empty doctrinarism, but a profound recognition of social principles, when they emphasized the alternative: private property or public property, capitalism or socialism. Indeed, for a society based on division of labor there are only these two possibilities; middle forms of organization are conceivable only in the sense that some means of production may be publicly owned while others are owned privately. But wherever property is in private hands, government intervention cannot eliminate the market price without simultaneously abolishing the regulating principle of production.

# THE NATIONALIZATION OF CREDIT?*

Arthur Travers-Borgstroem, a Finnish writer, published a book entitled *Mutualism* that deals with ideas of social reform, and culminates in a plea for the nationalization of credit. A German edition appeared in 1923. In 1917, the author had established a foundation under his name in Berne, Switzerland, whose primary objective was the conferring of prizes for writings on the nationalization of credit. The panel of judges consisted of Professors Diehl, Weyermann, Milhaud, and Reichesberg, the bankers Milliet, Somary, Kurz, and others. The judges awarded a prize to a paper submitted by Dr. Robert Deumer, director of the Reichsbank in Berlin. This paper was published in book form by the Mutualist Association of Finland.[1]

From the background material of the paper we can learn why the author is not concerned with the rationale of credit nationalization, but merely with the details of its realization. Dr. Deumer is presenting a proposal, elaborated in its insignificant details, on the nationalization of all German institutions of banking and credit, and the establishment of a national credit monopoly. But his plan can be of no inter-

---

* *Translator's note:* In his *Notes and Recollections* (South Holland, Ill.: Libertarian Press, 1977) the author revealed that he meant to include this essay—written in 1926—in the original German edition (1929). It was left out of that volume through editorial error, but was included in the 1976 German edition.

1. *Die Verstaatlichung des Kredits: Mutualisierung des Kredits* [Nationalization of credit: mutualization of credit], Prize Essay of the Travers-Borgstroem Foundation at Berne, Munich, and Leipzig, 1926.

est to us as no one is contemplating its implementation in the foreseeable future. And if there ever should be such a movement, conditions may be quite different so that the Deumer proposal will not be applicable. Therefore, it would not make any sense to discuss its details, such as article I, section 10, of the "Draft of a Bill Nationalizing Banking and Credit," which reads: "He who engages in any banking and credit transaction after the nationalization will be subject to a fine not exceeding ten million gold marks, or imprisonment up to five years, or both."[2]

Deumer's work is of interest to us because of its motives for the nationalization of credit, and its statements on a reform that preserves the superiority of "profit" management over "bureaucratic" management. These statements reveal an opinion that is shared by a large majority of our contemporaries, yes, that is even accepted without contradiction. If we should share this Deumer-Travers-Borgstroem-mutualist position we must welcome a nationalization of credit and every other measure leading to socialism. In fact, we must agree to its realizability and even its urgent necessity.

The public welcomes all proposals designed to limit the sphere of private property and entrepreneurship because it readily accepts the critique of the private property order by the Socialists of the Chair in Germany, the Solidarists in France, the Fabians in Great Britain, and the Institutionalists in the United States. If the nationalization proposals have not yet been fully realized we must not search for any opposition in social literature and the political parties. We must look to the fact that the public realizes that whenever enterprises are nationalized and municipalized or government otherwise interferes with economic life, financial failure and serious disruption of production and transportation follow instead of the desired consequences. Ideology has not yet taken stock of this failure of reality. It continues to hold fast to the desirability of public enterprises and the inferiority of private enterprises. And it continues to find only malice, selfishness, and ignorance in opposition to its

---

2. *Ibid.*, p. 335.

proposals, of which every objective observer should approve.

Under such conditions an analysis of Deumer's reasoning seems to be in order.

# 1.
# Private Interest
# and Public Interest

According to Deumer, banks presently serve private interests. They serve public interests only inasmuch as these do not conflict with the former. Banks do not finance those enterprises that are most essential from the national point of view, but only those that promise to yield the highest return. For instance, they finance "a whiskey distillery or any other enterprise that is superfluous for the economy." "From the national point of view, their activity is not only useless, but even harmful." "Banks permit enterprises to grow whose products are not in demand; they stimulate unnecessary consumption, which in turn reduces the people's purchasing power for goods that are more important culturally and rationally. Furthermore, their loans waste socially necessary capital, which causes essential production to decline, or at least their costs of credit, and thus their production costs, to rise."[3]

Obviously, Deumer does not realize that in a market order capital and labor are distributed over the economy in such a way that, except for the risk premium, capital yields the

---

3. *Ibid.*, p. 86.

same return, and similar labor earns the same wage everywhere. The production of "unnecessary" goods pays no more and no less than that of "essential goods." In the final analysis, it is the consumers in the market who determine the employment of capital and labor in the various industries. When the demand for an item rises its prices will rise and thus the profits, which causes new enterprises to be built and existing enterprises to be expanded. Consumers decide whether this or that industry will receive more capital. If they demand more beer, more beer will be brewed. If they want more classical plays, the theatres will add classics to their repertoire and offer fewer antics, slapstick, and operettas. The taste of the public, not the producer, decides that *The Merry Widow* and *The Garden of Eden* are performed more often than Goethe's *Tasso*.

To be sure, Deumer's taste differs from that of the public. He is convinced that people should spend their money differently. Many would agree with him. But from this difference in taste Deumer draws the conclusion that a socialistic command system should be established through nationalization of credit, so that public consumption can be redirected. On this we must disagree with Deumer.

Guided by central authority according to central plan, a socialistic economy can be democratic or dictatorial. A democracy in which the central authority depends on public support through ballots and elections cannot proceed differently from the capitalistic economy. It will produce and distribute what the public likes, that is, alcohol, tobacco, trash in literature, on the stage, and in the cinema, and fashionable frills. The capitalistic economy, however, caters as well to the taste of a few consumers. Goods are produced that are demanded by some consumers, and not by all. The democratic command economy with its dependence on popular majority need not consider the special wishes of the minority. It will cater exclusively to the masses. But even if it is managed by a dictator who, without consideration for the wishes of the public, enforces what he deems best, who clothes, feeds, and houses the people as he sees fit, there is no assurance that he will do what appears proper to "us." The critics of the capitalistic order always seem to believe that the socialistic system of their dreams will do precisely what they think correct. While they may not always count on becoming dictators themselves, they are hoping that the dictator will not act without first seeking their advice. Thus they arrive at the popular contrast of productivity and profitability. They call "productive" those economic actions they deem correct. And because things may be different at times they reject the capitalistic order which is guided by profitability and the wishes of consumers, the true masters of markets and production. They forget that a dictator, too, may act differently from their wishes, and that there is no assurance that he will really try for the "best," and, even if he should seek it, that he should find the way to the "best."

It is an even more serious question whether a dictatorship of the "best" or a committee of the "best" can prevail over the will of the majority. Will the people, in the long run, tolerate an economic dictatorship that refuses to give them what they want to consume and gives them only what the leaders deem useful? Will not the masses succeed in the end in forcing the leaders to pay heed to public wishes and taste and do what the reformers sought to prevent?

We may agree with Deumer's subjective judgment that the consumption by our fellow men is often undesirable. If we believe this we may attempt to convince them of their errors. We may inform them of the harm of excessive use of alcohol and tobacco, of the lack of value of certain movies, and of many other things. He who wants to promote good writings may imitate the example of the Bible Society that makes financial sacrifices in order to sell Bibles at reduced prices and to make them available in hotels and other public places. If this is yet insufficient, there cannot be any doubt that the will of our fellow men must be subdued. Economic production according to profitability means production according to the wishes of consumers, whose demand determines goods prices and thus capital yield and entrepreneurial profit. Whenever economic production according to "national productivity" deviates from the former, it means production that disregards the consumers' wishes, but pleases the dictator or committee of dictators.

Surely, in a capitalistic order a fraction of national income is spent by the rich on luxuries. But regardless of the fact that this fraction is very small and does not substantially affect production, the luxury of the well-to-do has dynamic effects that seem to make it one of the most important forces of economic progress. Every innovation makes its appearance as a "luxury" of the few well-to-do. After industry has become aware of it, the luxury then becomes a "necessity" for all. Take, for example, our clothing, the lighting and bathroom facilities, the automobile, and travel facilities. Economic history demonstrates how the luxury of yesterday has become today's necessity. A great deal of what people in the less capitalistic countries consider luxury is a common good in the more capitalistically developed countries. In Vienna, ownership of a car is a luxury (not just in the eyes of the tax collector); in the United States, one out of four or five individuals owns one.

The critic of the capitalist order who seeks to improve the conditions of the masses should not point at this luxury consumption as long as he has not disproved the assertion of theorists and the experience of reality that only capitalistic production assures highest possible production. If a command system produces less than a private property order it will obviously not be possible to supply the masses with more than they have today.

# 2.
# Bureaucratic Management or Profit Management of Banking?

The poor performance of public enterprises is usually blamed on bureaucratic management. In order to render state, municipal, and other public operations as successful

158

as private enterprise they should be organized and directed along commercial lines. This is why for decades everything has been tried to make such operations more productive through "commercialization." The problem became all the more important as state and municipal operations expanded. But not by a single step has anyone come closer to the solution.

Deumer, too, deems it necessary "to manage the national banking monopoly along commercial lines," and makes several recommendations on how to achieve this.[4] They do not differ from many other proposals in recent years or from those which under the circumstances could and have been achieved. We hear of schools and examinations, of promotion of the "able," of sufficient pay for employees, and of profit-sharing for leading officials. But Deumer does not see the essence of the problem any more clearly than do any others who seek to make the inevitably unproductive system of public operations more productive.

Deumer, in step with prevailing opinion, seems to believe erroneously that the "commercial" is a form of organization that can easily be grafted onto government enterprises in order to debureaucratize them. That which usually is called "commercial" is the essence of private enterprise aiming at nothing but the greatest possible profitability. And that which usually is called "bureaucratic" is the essence of government operations aiming at "national" objectives. A government enterprise can never be "commercialized" no matter how many external features of private enterprise are superimposed on it.

The entrepreneur operates on his own responsibility. If he does not produce at lowest costs of capital and labor what consumers believe they need most urgently, he suffers losses. But losses finally lead to a transfer of his wealth, and thus his power of control over means of production, to more capable hands. In a capitalistic economy the means of production are always on the way to the most capable manager, that is, to one who is able to use these means most economically to the satisfaction of consumer needs. A public enter-

---

4. *Ibid.*, p. 210.

prise, however, is managed by men who do not face the consequences of their success or failure.

The same is said to be true of the leading executives of large private enterprises which therefore are run as "bureaucratically" as state and municipal operations. But such arguments ignore the basic difference between public and private enterprises.

In a private, profit-seeking enterprise, every department and division is controlled by bookkeeping and accounting aiming at the same profit objective. Departments and divisions that are unprofitable are reorganized or closed. Workers and executives who fail in their assigned tasks are removed. Accounting in dollars and cents controls every part of the business. Monetary calculation alone shows the way to highest profitability. The owners, that is, the stockholders of a corporation, issue only one order to the manager who transmits it to the employees: earn profits.

The situation is quite different in the bureaus and courts that administer the affairs of the state. Their tasks cannot be measured and calculated in a way market prices are calculated, and the order given to subordinates cannot be so easily defined as that of an entrepreneur to his employees. If the administration is to be uniform and all executive power is not to be delegated to the lowest officials, their actions must be regulated in every detail for every conceivable case. Thus it becomes the duty of every official to follow these instructions. Success and failure are of lesser importance than formal observance of the regulation. This is especially visible in the hiring, treatment, and promotion of personnel, and is called "bureaucratism." It is no evil that springs from some failure or shortcoming of the organization or the incompetency of officials. It is the nature of every enterprise that is not organized for profit.

When state and municipality go beyond the sphere of court and police, bureaucratism becomes a basic problem of social organization. Even a profit-seeking public enterprise could not be unbureaucratic. Attempts have been made to eliminate bureaucratism through profit-sharing by managers. But since they could not be expected to bear the eventual losses, they are tempted to become reckless, which then is to be avoided by limiting the manager's authority through directives from higher officials, boards, committees, and "expert" opinions. Thus again, more regulation and bureaucratization are created.

But usually public enterprises are expected to strive for more than profitability. This is why they are owned and operated by government. Deumer, too, demands of the nationalized banking system that it be guided by national rather than private considerations, that it should invest its funds not where the return is highest, but where they serve the national interest.[5]

We need not analyze other consequences of such credit policies, such as the preservation of uneconomical enterprises. But let us look at their effects on the management of public enterprises. When the national credit service or one of its branches submits an unfavorable income statement it may plead: "To be sure, from the viewpoint of private interest and profitability we were not very successful. But it must be borne in mind that the loss shown by commercial accounting is offset by public services that are not visible in the accounts. For instance, dollars and cents cannot express our achievements in the preservation of small and medium enterprises, in the improvements of the material conditions of the 'backbone' classes of population." Under such conditions the profitability of an enterprise loses significance. If public management is to be audited at all, it must be judged with the yardstick of bureaucratism. Management must be regimented, and positions must be filled with individuals who are willing to obey the regulations.

No matter how we may search, it is impossible to find a form of organization that could prevent the strictures of bureaucratism in public enterprises. It won't do to observe that many large corporations have become "bureaucratic" in recent decades. It is a mistake to believe that this is the result of size. Even the biggest enterprise remains immune to the dangers of bureaucratism as long as it aims exclusively at

---

5. *Ibid.,* p. 184.

profitability. True, if other considerations are forced on it, it loses the essential characteristic of a capitalistic enterprise. It was the prevailing etatistic and interventionistic policies that forced large enterprises to become more and more bureaucratic. They were forced, for instance, to appoint executives with good connections to the authorities, rather than able businessmen, or to embark upon unprofitable operations in order to please influential politicians, political parties, or government itself. They were forced to continue operations they wished to abandon, and merge with companies and plants they did not want. The mixing of politics and business not only is detrimental to politics, as is frequently observed, but even much more so to business. Many large enterprises must give thousands of considerations to political matters, which plants the seeds of bureaucratism. But all this does not justify the proposals to bureaucratize completely and formally all production through the nationalization of credit. Where would the German economy be today if credit had been nationalized as early as 1890, or even 1860? Who can be aware of the developments that will be prevented if it is nationalized today?

# 3.
# The Danger of Overexpansion and Immobilization

What has been said here applies to every attempt at transferring private enterprises, especially the banking system, into the hands of the state, which in its effects would amount to all-round nationalization. But in addition, it would create credit problems that must not be overlooked.

Deumer seeks to show that the credit monopoly could not be abused for fiscal reasons. But the dangers of credit nationalization do not lie here; they lie with the purchasing power of money.

As is well known, demand deposits subject to checks have the same effect on the purchasing power of a monetary unit as bank notes. Deumer even proposes an issue of "guaranteed certificates" or "clearing house certificates" that are never to be redeemed.[6] In short, the national bank will be in the position to inflate.

Public opinion always wants "easy money," that is, low interest rates. But it is the very function of the note-issuing bank to resist such demands, protecting its own solvency and maintaining the parity of its notes toward foreign notes and gold. If the bank should be excused from the redemption of its certificates it would be free to expand its credits in accordance with the politicians' wishes. It would be too weak to resist the clamor of credit applicants. But the banking system is to be nationalized, in Deumer's words, "to pay heed to the complaints of small industrial enterprises and many commercial firms that they are able to secure the necessary credits only with great difficulties and much sacrifice."[7]

A few years ago it would have been necessary to elaborate the consequences of credit expansion. There is no need for such an effort today. The relationship between credit expansion and rising goods prices and foreign exchange rates is well known today. This has been brought out not only by the research of some economists, but also by the American and British experiences and theories with which Germans have become familiar. It would be superfluous to elaborate further on this.

---

6. *Ibid.*, p. 152 *et seq.*
7. *Ibid.*, p. 184.

# 4.
# Summation

Deumer's book clearly reveals that etatism, socialism, and interventionism have run their course. Deumer is unable to support his proposals with anything but the old etatist and Marxian arguments which have been refuted a hundred times. He simply ignores the critique of these arguments. Nor does he consider the problems that arose from recent socialistic experience. He still takes his stand on the ground of an ideology that welcomes every nationalization as progress, even though it has been shaken to its foundations in recent years.

Politics, therefore, will ignore Deumer's book, which may be regrettable from the author's viewpoint because he invested labor, ingenuity, and expertise in his proposals. But in the interest of a healthy recovery of the German economy, it is gratifying.